BOOK OF A THOUSAND POEMS

by

Christian McDonough

D.F.L.
LIT
LAPSUS SURSUM

THE FIRST 100 POEMS

1

We shall begin it, this book,
Here.

Yet it shall begin again, a hundredfold.
And with each beginning a new task
To be accomplished.

You shall see all things overcome,
Your self shattered,
Your world remade.

And me?
Perhaps I will become nothing.
Perhaps I will become everything.
I'm sure I'll hate and love and all the rest,
And generally be,
a bit of this and a bit of that
For all to see.

And the book?
The book shall be everything.
Shall be you, I, the world, and the new world,
Even God.

A simple mess.
A leisure, a little blessing.
A fine reprieve from everything...

Oh...! To be free!
We can be babies.

A distraction, too.
          Perhaps even an escape...

It can be sad sometimes
But that is what it takes.

It is here! We are here!
To see that the world may be remade.
To see that that which we take as true, as complete, is not even set.
To know that we may create & recreate
All.

To make you everything
To show you your beauty
To hold you and love you and care for you
To make you my everything
To give you everything
I do it all for you
I love...Oh God! I love you...

The First 100 Poems

The creature slowly rises
Me! I am its master!
I am happy to hold my baby
And fuck it and kill it
And resurrect it again
Here
For all to see

6

This shall be myself
This shall be all that I am
All that I am shall be exposed, emptied
So that it may be seen
      So that it may be overcome

Complete, total honesty
Complete and total confession

The end of history
The end of my lesson

"I," a figment
A tragic ligament

A careless, covered slate
To be emptied,
To be *made* blank

To rid you of
The dandy "ubermensch"
The wandering toe on a bench
The supreme idiot
The blasphemous "-mensch"

No one will be here
No one will be there

Your body will decompose
The hands will shake
Liquified, your eyes
The pupils dilate
And bubble over
And dissipate

Your legs, the bones,
They'll crumble into themselves
While your skin holds it in place
You'll crumble and fumble

You shall be made a goop, a mass
An un-kempt thing
Put into its place

To determine from life
What life we must live
What person we must be
What things we must say

To know our new morality
And do what we "must" do

But it is all so dark
And so empty

Can it really be done?
Should it?
Why?
And why not!

9

To betray the world
To inflict my will upon it
To kill you
To kill myself

That is why I will write
That is why I will be
I will end it
I will end it all

To protect myself

10

The dirt, shit, and garbage will be seen.
It will be heard.
It will, finally, be known.

Alas, but who am I?
To flounder in the mud?
To wash in babe's blood?

But a whimper!
A piss!
A little, brittle,
Shit!

To read this book is to let your face be shoved into the mud…
(and blood and shit and piss and fuck and cum and death and wretch)
Will you allow such a simple test?

What will you make of it?
Haha! I ask you, I beg you, to hate it!

11

13

It begins, so it will end.
The life and death
Of a million bastards.
Infinity in fucks.
This place a home
For a true life.
A real life.

This place of birth
For what is to come.
And what will be
Here, within.

12

A tactile experience
Of flesh, blood, and bone
The scent, a bitterness, an acrid- ...A burning...
  Breathing in deep and the...
  The wash of foul feet, in the mind seeing
  A little bundle of weedy sticks,
  A cow on a ranch, a "white picket fence"
And to touch...
  To touch and to feel...
  There is pressure, softness, comfort
  The comfort of love, physical
  A body plunged into without blood
  Everything almost pain
  The body enclosed, crushed
  A knock at one's knee, the stinging
  As if ringing!
To hear the words
And know them
   Ooooooooooo
   Aaaaaaaaaaa
   Quea
   Coro-o-o-o-
A siren calling out as the waves crash
Black night against the beach, the sand
Still, wet, grain falling between the fingers
Everything against the ears
And-

Oh! I get ahead of myself
Much too far
Ahead of myself...

To fade away
And be new again
To remake myself
Again and again

So that I might see something else
So that I might be someone else

And finally escape
But also renew

Everyone and everything
All that I see
To be all that I can be

And never know! Never, never know!
Only see and hear and all the rest
Just here, making myself into
A horrible mess

To make you cower in fear
To make you shrivel like a raisin
Ah, ah, to be above you
To tower over you
To make you know that you are nothing
To make you, finally, into something...

Christian McDonough

Here...? We are here...?
To show...?
To say...?
What!?
Anything?
Everything?
To question...
We are here to question...
To ponder...
To see the mysteries.
To know that we do not know.
A ghastly visage,
Is all that might be shown...
And, God fucking bless it!
It is so!

To create
          And to be with God.
I blow apart my body by writing to you now
I sacrifice myself for this
I am made into pieces.

Pure and true creation
          A total ambition
A magnificent giant
          A horrible tyrant...

I blaspheme and seem
To myself, supreme

I create and am gone
And am gone and am here
And here, with God
I am nothing but a piece
Of a greater puzzle
Of an infinite struggle.

There, here, and elsewhere
The truth and fragility
Of all things
Is.

And here
          Not there
We come together
To stare

The creation of a world
Of a meaning
Of a "Way"

Here,
Where it all begins
Where it all ends
Your life
And all other's lives

The new life begins
The life of something else
Of "Something,"
And of nothing (haha)

We will not know, nor see
We will only be?

No.
And yes.

18

To create "Actions"
Things to be done
Instructions for life
Possible events
For multiple to share
A collective experience
A shove, a dare...

19

To spit in the face of God
To make him beg for forgiveness
To make him suffer like I have
To kill him again
To crucify him
To end him eternally
"He" is the one that holds it all?
"He" is the one that has made it so?
"He" is beauty? "He" is truth?

What has beauty given us?
And what of truth?

The end of "Him" allows the future,
The "true" future,
To begin.

Freedom, ecstasy, creation, negation
Beginnings and Ends
Answers and Questions

Together, with this book,
With You & I,
We can achieve
We can complete
We can become
       And overcome

All

To reach out to others
To make friends

I don't want to be alone
I want to be heard
And seen
And felt
And thought of

I yearn for someone
I wish for you

Will you read this?
Will you be with me?
Will you care for me?

And I will care for you.

To learn about you
To speak with you
To hear you
To know you
To have a conversation

Please

All to feel
Hate, love, fear, peace,
To feel all
Being, dying, living,
It, and all,
To be
To see

To know
And to hold
And to give away
To leave
And return
And begin
And end

For the sake of itself
For the sake of something
Just to have it
To have done it

To create a new religion
For all to profit from
(But mostly me)

I will have you all!
I will have you all!
I will be all for you!
And, yes, be nothing for you (praise be)

To be and be and be
To let it all be followed and lived as it should
(All, as it should)
To make a way for so that it shall be as it is *to be*
(And moreso)

And ever so
And on, so
Againe...

For no reason
For no rhyme!
Only teasing
Only passing time.
I cannot know
Why a thing is done,
I only try
And try
And try
And try
And try
And try...

To recreate a sacred past
A sacred space
A sacred place

To roar about in that strange night
Where the devils, creatures, and critters are aflight

Where the laughing witch
Doth give one a fright
And the crackling flames
Burn O so bright!

A great, forgotten past!
An intangibility!
An impossibility!

To see and be, beyond time and space
Into that thing,
The most sacred space

For there a new world is seen
A new possibility
A new "obscene"

A majestic thing
To be there alone
A long, long time ago

And to know it now

And...
And to be it...
To...
To do...
I...
I don't know!

It! It!
"Tragedy" and "Boundless"!

And the words all fall away.

To learn of who I am and might be
To look deep within and see
Finally, me

Me, me, me, me, me, me, me

To only care for me
To help me
To "process trauma"
To "overcome adversity"

All done here, with me
And Me

Forsooth, to see.

To create new worlds
Infinite worlds
Where everything is different
And completely new thoughts
And new creation
Is possible

To tell the tale
Of all tales
The story
Which must be heard

To tell of stories
Which answer the worlds
And show and educate
What must be known

The human soul...
The endless possibility...

Of what is here and there
And what one can be

To tell it and show it
And let it be known

To shake you!
To make you...!

These stories...
Those stories...

Which unearth it all again

To bring peace to all
To be a comfort
To be kind

I am here so that I might be that for you
Oh, to be with you
Like a great tidal wave
I wash over
And the brine rises, the foam foams!

O-ah-O-Ah!
That blessed
That cursed
That dainty thing!

World peace!
An end to suffering!

31

To make the evil hurt.
To Destroy.

I will crush their nuts beneath my bootheel!
I will turn their mountains into molehills!
I am the one, true deliverance
Of justice.

It is still beginning
It is still coming in to being
And that is where it may be seen:
In between.

In between, in the middle,
There is something coming,
Something going.

Isn't it lovely to see?

Oh, it is lovely to see.

A person may speak to me
And just to hear their voice
Is a divine ecstasy.

I do not want to hurt you
But I know that I must,
I know that I will.

31

Here, where we are now
We can stand from above
And gaze at what we will soon encounter

The hills, the peaks and valleys
The dark wood, the foggy marsh

And deep within
Tiny, infantile things
Babes and bitches
Creepies and crawlies
Sticks and stones

Praise be that they be
For soon we shall see
And know
What it is that they have meant

For us
For them

It is

And it is coming
And soon enough we shall go away
And even beyond

32

With all this I might get away
I might allow my anger to subside
And dissipate.
Oh, such anger
And for no real purpose
To no real end.

Hatred, only to hate
I hate the world
I hate its people
I hate what is said
I hate how they care

I want them dead, deep inside, dead
I want them all like me
And then, all death.

Yes, all death.

But no, let it end.
And let me love them.

Perhaps I could love them.
I want to love them.
I will never love them?
But we shall see soon enough.

By God, I might change.

33

If only to see my own face.

To see it twist and turn.

My dramatic poise:
I wallow in sadness,
My lips downturned.
My brows furrowed, oh, so tense.
A whistle from my wet lips.
And a coo, too.

My cheeks sunken in,
My face perfect.

And a laughing face,
A big smile!
A mouth of teeth,
Two or three slightly crooked,

And a mouth of teeth,
Jaw wired shut.

From deep within my throat,
A guttural *guffaw*.
If only to see a new look,
A stupid look,
A banal,
A carnal,
A trivial

Mug.

I shall remake you all.
I shall remake everything.

Yet, and yet,
We live to be
And see

We live and live
For this here and there
This life
Given by all
By existence
(What is God?)
And what is it that is here?
(Plants, rocks, animals, etc.)

Yes, yet, and yet, and so
We are here (in this book)
To say and do
All that we can
In the face of it all
God, in the face of it,
Oh, god.

I am here. Not you.
I am here to say things,
To show all that I know,
To show how big and strong I am.
Look at me, oh wow.

The First 100 Poems

I speak, I speak to speak
I write to say
To be heard
But really to speak

To speak so that speaking may speak
So that it may continue
Thoughts
In words
Out

Here, there,
So that they might go on

You see,
Words, spoken, go on and on
And create something
Just by speaking
And it shows me something
And someone might be there to hear it
And perhaps they too will speak
And go on and on
Speaking

This book too
Might be only to
Reach inside myself,
This creature that I am,
And pull out the dark viscera
Which taints me
Which haunts me

The black nothingness inside me
The everlasting pain burned into me

Yes, to "retraumatize"
And, to "detraumatize"

To show the hate and suffering
And the pain inflicted and taken
      To overcome this
      To simply have it out, again

With the fading hope
That it might result
In something different

Yet here, still
I shall throw away the past
I shall forget all
I shall be new again

It is here where I,
Perhaps we,
May unmake our sour souls!
Might outpour the pools of our minds,
Lightly reach in to our brained cavities
          And remove the soft insides

And look! Lo! Behold!
          Those pink mushy masses!
That we called, once, a God!

And a pleasant, dumb fuck nothing!
A little "retard," in the vat of something...

The book is a farce,
A joke, a jape.
A big and little mistake.

It will be made and remade and unmade.
It will be taken and seen,
Judged, with hate.

It is done for no reason
Or for any reason at all.

It is wasteful and empty,
Dull, banal.

Yet there too
Is something
In the nothing
Of the banal

Yet there is something
Necessary
To hold
To crawl

It is always there
The endless
Stupid
Abyss
Of shit

And yet another purpose
Yet another reason
Another ghost

There...!

In the stall.

Down, deep down
There, we might find
Something untrue,
And yet,
Divine.

There we will search
And hope to see

The devils and demons

Of yesterday's screed.

And perhaps then know
What must be done

Today,
Here,
In the light of the sun.

Even now!
To kill!
To devour!

All!

To make shit of good taste
And in their face
Place a horrible disgrace.

To cut them open
And tear out their guts,
To rub them upon
My great big nuts.

Yes, yes...
Even this is yet to come.

Please now stay.
Soon enough,
We will have fun...

To finally show them
The ill of their ways.

You & I!
Together!
We'll take them away!

Their shit, their detritus,
Will finally be cleansed.

Again, aghast,
They will finally see

That they are hurting,
That they cause pain,
That they are the ones

With tumors in their brains.

And then we will rise!
Up! Above it all!

And they will collapse,
Oh yes,
They will fall.

45

It is also...
Only to show...
And tease and bring...
About such beautiful things...

Oh, to feel,
To know,
To see
What is there.

Only to be something beautiful,
To be something cared for,
To be tender and true...

To be delicate.
To be with you!
Oh, please, yes, with you!

I only want
You to see
Oh, how much...
You mean...
To me.

It is that "classical" kind of thing...
The pursuit of truth,
Of beauty.
"A treatise on what it means to be human."

Yes, something trite,

But still it prevails.
The pursuit of it all,
Of your life,
How it calls...

It is what it must be.
To know because it is good,
To praise the good, good world,
To become a poet.

Because my life is so important,
Because my thoughts are so pure.

Ah, yes, because I am
The world.

The book shall show
        And become
A gateway, a passage

Into the greatest of absurdities
Into the worst of creation

For within we shall find
A whole new world!
A whole new way!
A whole new self!
A new beginning!

All perhaps today

Yes.

It is a creation
Like a monster
A homunculus...
Whose body trembles and shakes
Whose bones ache
As life slowly arises
From without
From within

As our pure electricity
Our virile life
Is injected
Fucked
Into it
All

And the world shall be lived in
And we shall be whole within

Christian McDonough

We shall offer up such sacrifices...
Such tender things...

Our time,
Our mind,
Our life given freely,

All so that it may be and become
What it is
And what it was.

Yes, our pasts too,
Shall be here
In this book.

All that we once were,
All that we might be,
Contained, perhaps hidden,
Within
And between
Each page.

To answer, finally,
Those fundamental questions...
What is life's purpose?
Does God exist?
What is our nature?
What is the nature of existence? Of being?
What are we?
What principles, axioms, does the world rely upon?
What is reality?
What is the mind?
What of our will?
Our freedom?
What is right?
And what is wrong?

To blow away! O- aha!
To blow away these prejudices of knowledge!
These preconceptions we hold so dear!

That to find truth one must speak truthfully,
One must speak clearly, obscurely, "smartly"! Paha!

Away! Away with it all!

We shall find every answer in every way!
For that is the only way,
To know it every which way,
And hold it
And see it
And do every single fucking thing we can to it!

51

We shall finally find
(and perhaps even fund)
The correct way to govern,
To live life as a country,
To know what must be done.

And how.
And when.

To answer the questions
Of the common,
Of all women,
And all men.

54

To confront death
And see that it can be beautiful
And fulfilling
And an answer
And an end
Which brings something great
Which finally makes sense of it all
Which finally shows you
What you are
What you were
What they were
What they did
What happened
And what is
Possibly
To come

I will show you
True morality
And perhaps grant us
A kind of immortality

The way we must act
The way we must speak
The way we must think

All that we *must* be

The real point
Is just
To talk
About
Trees

55

To experience time
As it passes
As it recurs
To make it last a million nights
Within a single word

To make it abreast
Of itself
And of the clouds
And the past
And beyond
Its own
Everything

You see
Time dissolves
And hardens

It can be an infinity
Within the infinitesimal

It is a true mystery
And key

To the great questions
Like the ones
We will soon answer

To create incantations
Words
Which will bring out the dead
And make them move again

The dead shall live
Here
In these words

And all life shall be in jeopardy

As it should be

And you will know it
And feel it
From deep within

To make the afterlife
Live with life
To make the life before life
The life which we may live

To bring Nirvana
To bring all Seven Hells

To make a pilgrimage
To the great ends
Beyond the Absurd

To cast final judgment
On all who have lived

To find the final words
Which must be said

For there
For there

It will then be known

Who is who
And what
And when

To say simply
That I saw this then
Or did this at that time

So that someone might know
That I am, or was, alive

And just to reorient
Myself in my world

Knowing that I did do something that day
To get out of my head
And think about something else

To show that nothing can be known
That no answers can be given
And that any pursuit of such a task
Is mistaken,
Cruel, and dim,
For there is nothing that can be said clearly
And nothing that can be communicated
From one to another
For we are always lost in confusion
And always trapped within our selves

63

To remind you
To look out
At what is in front of you

To crack open the culture
So that its deep, fateful desires
Might spool out into the open
So that it might finally be seen
For what it truly is

63

To bring about such moments
As those under the Sun and Moon
Where one looks out with their eyes
And sees with their mind
The coalescence
Of the past and future
Of what has physical form
And what is formless

Those moments in which
A greater sense
A Logos
Is known

To perhaps make my hero
Stanislaw Ignacy Witkiewicz
Proud

So that he might look down upon me
From on high
And smile
Then snicker
Then burst out with a laugh
Pointing at me
And buckling over
With a vicious glee

To form a group of followers
Who might all care for one another
And work together
Toward something

Something creative
Something beautiful
Something real

To abandon humanity
To leave people
To get away from them
Because they fill me with such hatred
Because they know such stupidity

To escape them and then
To be alone
To be lost within the work
And still have everything

To find humanity in the work itself
To find even more to abandon

To finally reach the point
Of ultimate idiocy
To become God's little idiot
God's little bastard

That is who I am
That is who I want to be

But only through this creation
May I finally reach it

To show the experience
The process
The truth
Of becoming

To show how it can be done
To show what it means
To make it obey

To show the experience of meaning making,
To let meaning have its way...

For meaning can be so mysterious,
But so meaningful!

It can be clear.

If only we bring it out again

And then you can hold it,
And know it...

It's for you,
My friend.

To break the curse of rationality
To push beyond that limit

So that a true freedom of thought may be attained
And all the children may sing

Christian McDonough

To make the body disappear
So that your fears may disappear as well
To provide you comfort outside of your own skin
To bring the body to its point of collapse
And let what is inside come out

To create new internal processes of thought
To create new structures within the self
So that completely new approaches
To the world, to society, to politics, to being,
May be made
And may reinvigorate
All possibilities

To show that all things
Are of equal value
Even people
Even plants
Even thoughts
Even time

All contributes to all
In equal measure

And all is dependent upon all
At every point

To make the thing
That all people long for

To complete the task
That creation has begun

The First 100 Poems

77

To end philosophy
Once and for all

Whatever that might mean!

...

Well, soon enough,
I suppose we'll see.

To help us reach mental states
Which themselves are answers
To all eternal questions

To show that there are always things missing
That there is always something forgotten
And that life never serves itself so freely
As to allow you the chance
At an eternity of anything

To create an eternity
Upon every page

An infinity of possibility
As times recur
Without age

Yes, to blacken out the eternal
And make it my own

For this eternity
Is beyond all known

81

For the cucocala
As it vanquishes the blood

And the foie ve cao
For it unmakes all floods

With the dangers inherent,
The book still made
With the greatest of intent:

To make the bed again.

Where then it shall lay,
The wolf in its chambers,

And finally, finally,
It can start to come
Into play.

For my dog
For my family
For my future wife and child

For my friends
For my feet
For my hidden lowly desires

For them and others
I write this troublesome tome

If nothing else
For them alone

To find my spirit
And shake it loose!
To play at hanging
Myself from a noose.

The First 100 Poems

To hurt other people
To make them feel bad
Because they deserve it
Because they are bad

86

To make Nietzsche like me
He wrote some poems too
To make him say,
"Gee. I guess that'll do."

And maybe even David Lynch too
He's still alive
I could write this book
And he might not yet have died

And for the book
For it called to me too
It wishes for life
It thinks it is destined
It thinks it has a right

To get away from the internet
And from TV.
Oh,
But the internet,
How it disgusts me.

To catch sight of a ghost...
Or a goblin...
Or a ghoul...

When I was a child...
How I wished it be true...

To pretend that I
Am good at things

Like sports
Or working

Good, common things

Then I'll show them
My big book
And they'll give me
Jobs and money

And I won't ever have to worry about anything

To finally enjoy
Something
In this shit life

Christian McDonough

To find a reason
To believe in something

Be it god
Or the world
Or a person
Or a people

To find a reason
And maybe many reasons

And then
To have faith

To take all of my shit
And shove it in a place
Where it might not be met
As a total disgrace

To love my parents
To somehow make them understand
That I am doing something

That they can look at
And smile at
And be happy with

Something like that

Made

By my own hand

94

To make my parents ecstatic
Upon seeing something
That is my own
That I have written

Something that will truly move them
And truly fill them
With pride
For me
Their oldest son

To make something
That my parents can't excuse themselves
From reading

To not be alone
And not be sad
And not be angry
When I look at you

The First 100 Poems

99

To be ok again
And comfort myself
And accept that I
Can't stop myself

To finally accept others as they are
And not be filled with rage when I hear them
Say that they think something
That I don't like
That I think is dumb
That makes me insecure
That makes me want to die

And to just be there
Here
In the world
And be ok with it
Even if it's horrible
Or something
Like that

To forgive
And move on
Past the woman
Who treated me
In such a way
That I hated her
And my life
And everything
And was hurt
In such a way
That I can't stop thinking about her
That I can't stop hating her
That she still fucks my life
Though she's long gone

And now, finally,
All of this, all that I have proposed,
All that we have begun to yearn for
Can now
At long last
Begin
To become

The First 100 Poems

SOUP

101

Dkeimennirepatalatoratamunitobegaritofuckinimobeniggggoooooottttteres patatapetitamunolaQoutrimnentoparlinoutmainintoraliniaintingoftheresel lomuntaliopornographiotomakinomeetomeatrressuntapourificantesaroniq uoamazestunderfagrotritificialicalitopourintedsalliconemaycacurachacoot odealofignmuntiporificassfuckoreapature

Gull
Hog
Foss
Ilized

Soup

Nigger
Kike
Spic
Faggot
Retard
Wop
Paki
Cunt
Gook
Mick
Cracker

The erudite reaching
Of one Whom
Everso belonging upon
That which we now
May see with
Such and such
For such and such
In light of
Great findings
Of unknown origins
Due to the reckoning
Of that which

Fate-cum
Orange-Red
Jesus-bear
Lion- under-
"Non-"

Haggard weave-ling
Traitor
Back and before
Became it self
Again

113

Anus torn
Ripped
Fucked
And bloodied

A crack
A tear
A hole

Fire flame
Acrimonious languor
What which be
Witch witch witch

Sly upon its tits

Le flame arise
To and toward
Ah, ack!
To
Back

Click, snap, crack, creak
Eek, drip, woosh, shh
Ahh, huh, hunh, tut
Whistle, rumble, rustle

116

Rub, stroke, push, shove
Hump, jump, fall, dive
Punch, poke, fondle, tease
Grab, hold, release, cum
Lay, hang, swing, dangle
Walk, run, move, sit
Wait, stop, reach

A red fish
A blue fish
Two fish
Salty, sweet
Raw, bitter
Smooth, rich

Stick, brown
Little twig
Snapped ends,
Bumps

Smells shitty

And pissy

And pussy

And stench of man

And stench of woman

Something off, something decomposing
Rotting,
Rotten eggs, Gasoline,
Acrid, burning, stinging

Soup

Tracking tracing trailing tra-
To tot teet tut
Man becomes woman
Woman becomes man
Horticulture be hung
Yet yet yet yet

HATE! HATE! HATE! HATE!
LOVE!
Nothing...
Note...
Fate...

A gimp legged boy-man

I reached for the handle...!
Oh, but to reach for *that!*
Strength and vigor
Restless
Untouched

122

A taint is cunted
A cunt is pated

117

Shoom shoom shoom shoom
Within within within
Inside! Inside! Inside!

Then there then was when

It-

124

A noose
A hangman
A gag

Soup

125

Feral orifice
Pots' pear
Harangue
Quiver
Quotidian belligerent
Bucking bastille

A corpulence
A cropulence
Un- fang
Der tod
Trepanned
Bung
Hole

127

Muntraynet
Become-et
Voluptuous
Mon cure

A word
A whisper
A silent
Kiss

Soup

Nagging feeling
Toothing at it
And peeling it
Scratching
'Til pure

130

Wastebasket
Sidled

And refuse
All hanging
Aloft

125

A pussyfoot
A bondage
Leather
Strapped
Smothered
Confined

Weasel skitters up
Into the anus
Mouth ajar
A hunger
A thirst

Faces
Big & small
Noses cracked and turning

Mouths eyes
Eyes mouth

Bulging
Popping
Melding
Coming

134

Lalalala lala lala lala
Peace in fog
Lololololo lalo lola
Run through bog

Man & woman
Spear
Heart-carcass
Flesh-dome

Toward reckoning
Ahhh...
The mouth open
The mount mounted

Whore dish
Nymph tongue
Skybox
Empire

Eels slipping through
Heavy thick slime
Crackling energy
Zap-zapping spine

139

Of all time
Great hero
Good job
Smiling man

Tree
Thick and brown
Strong
Green
Full
Alone

A slice of line
In darkness
A twine
String gathered
And diapered
Puff patties
In the absence

...

142

Doctor
Mad scientist
Lab coat
Face upturned
Mouth open
Creation
Inspiration
Eureka

Spidery gate
Opens slow
Thunder and lightning
Dark clouds overhead
Theremin twang
Ghost sang
Something coming

Boogie woogie

Hairs and goats
A crocodile man
Face with a maw
Several severed hands

Cowgirl
In the sun
Having fun
Riding hard
Working
Large breasts

146

Sallow gaunt holes
Sewn shut mouths
Pus and festering
Aching
Burning
Yearning

Reaching hands
Reaching to touch
To grab and hold
The light shining
Too bright

Fear
Chittering teeth
Biting hands and wrists
Bleeding
Cutting
For, for, for,

A white throne
A white dress
A maiden woman
A homely guest

Acting a failing
A failure a flower
Aching ah fuck

151

Big man penis
For others

(Not for me!)

152

To the as one
For if it be none
Some other or two
Flight over under free
I, you, to and from
The beginning
The end
Undone

Red eyes
Widowed lips
Half cut
Sunken cheeks
Shining darkly
Perfect teeth

154

Soft curved face
Half a heart
An embrace

Blee blee blee!
Young hippee!
Untrundled bunghole
Flung dang fang

Wash wash watch
Hang clock hand
Minute minute
Running man

Simple rot
Across compounded
Hill and trough
Pivot pivot
Uncoupling

Silent girl
Little dress
Hand a mess
Butter made
Crapped bloody
Cake

159

Mustache man
Hand in pocket
Hair too long
Drink in hand
Walking head
Just above sand

Simple bench
Dirty ground
Concrete
Grass
Wood chips
Bushes
People
Babies
Blankets
Garbage
Thieves
Helpers
Alcoholics
Beer
Music

For the true
And real purpose
Of

It was there
And its fangs...!

What is
That
Ove-

164 Soup

A completion
For the goal
Which now lets us
Become
That thing
Which is

...

Trap

...

Love
Hate
Fear
Sorrow
Disgust
Shame
Pride

Faioauta
PLOIMKACIXZ
sumauiotanp
QeVwAbHwU
WBFZsdrk

Charmwell poisedrain toilpiss legdrops massviola dreamhold
Querytaste lionbane poisondiet regurgitatediverted
Neverfunnel huntergrain lovehushtrail wusspussling wastenumb

A B C D E F G
H I J K L M N O P
Q R S
T U V
W X
Y
Z

Red red red red
Black black black black
Numb
Yellow yellow green
Purple black pink
Feign
Thumb

Sadness looming
Great wings
Leather flapping
Sky burns

172

Infinity encounters
Men and women
Eyes wash over
Lives alter

Human feeling
Thrown away
Great life underneath
Above all

Power attained
For power
Hangings
Goodness
As an act
Become real

Impossible reaching
Necessity of achievement
Infinity
Change

Time over
Breach
Crack
Past & Future

177

All thought
Altered
All

Altered

172

Trailing land
Unfiltered air
Degradation
Disgust
Illness
Blood

Headless woman
Body like a man
She speaks
Acephalous

Collective thought
New reaction
Malignant psychology

Traitor & betrayal
Love & sex
Disgust & recoil
Bondage & domination

Soup

Metaphysics
Ended
Remade
Unmade
Torn

183

God
As a farce
For the impossible
Done with
And again

Living
For nothing
Necessities
Reassigned
Compartmentalized
Regrouped

Soup

Savage life
Loved
And lived
Again

Modernity
Hollowed
And praised
A tube
Split through
Tiny chunks
Sent

Horror and pain
For everyone
Again
And again

Everything
For everyone
With & without
Distractions
Eliminated

Milk
Broccoli
Egg
Sugar

Gat
Cat
Tata
Taca

Gata Gaga Caca

191

Daffodil
Rose
Peony
Lily

Travel
Trial
Final
Sow

Acceptance
All
Kindness
Love
Care
Tender

Tit squeeze
Squash nub
Limb numb
Agog agog

Production ended
No means
No end

Which is as
Ever the blatant
Relegation to one
Of the sort
That

197

Being eternal
And true
It was

Hell & Heaven
Heads in ass
Fugged the bunt
Ragged the cat

Traitorous feelings
Dealing Hung Dry
Uncoupled the mealing
The Worms Inside

Shhh
Ah sissy
You silent
Dumb missy

Flight
Of conquest
No fancy
For freedom

Loin liver lolly
Dirty bastard Polly
Untainted Unheld
Freedom of folly

Waste
Regurgitates
Bat paste

Nihill
Redoubled
And Prometheus
Fingered

Crack
Of a joke
And shiver
And Fumble

Never and never
Again and again
The lion
The bee
The ever of end

Soup

LIFE

I.
"I"…?
What?
"What?"
Who?
"Who?"
I, and who am I?
Here,
I am?
Everything,
Here.
No "I."
I and I and I and…
You.
You & I.
Us.
We.
Together.
All.

I am not I, yet I am. And I live. And you live.
We live, all of us.
All of it.
Everything alive.
I see it all.
And it is here.
Look & see.
That which is beyond, and plantlike, and animal…
And to reach and to touch and to know,
But never to know…
That which is contained within.
Within me?

Living

We see a scene play out before us:
>   None speak to us,
>   None know us,
>   And we feel we are helpless before it.

(It would only take a word,
A single action...

To throw ourselves deep into the lives
Of all around us.)

213

To reflect...
Oh, it's so strange.
To speak.
Oh, it's so strange.
That there,
And this here.

Uncanny...

Unknowable...

There are times when the heart beats fast,
The body curls up into itself,
Holds itself
Like an animal.

One can barely move.
One can barely think.
All one can do
Is breathe.

A thousand lives,
A thousand deaths,

And still, we might never know...
Why is it so?

Is one a doll?
Or is one a lion?

With breasts like a chicken's?
Or balls like a stallion's?

The talons cut deep
And sink themselves in

Let these words be a call
To the you deep within.

We can rise up
And reach up…

Stillness can be held
In such moments.

And the things we thought
We could not do,

Are soon enough
Already done.

To look with intention...
My oh my!
And with intention...
To see.
And that which we see...
Is...
Is...
There!

And there, we make it so.
And there, we are a thousand things.
And we close it all to one.

Life

The bobcat hunts its prey.

The spider spins its web.

The plant grows.

The stars turn.

When we do not see,
When we close our eyes,
We are made brilliant.

Or not.

We are kaleidoscopic...?

We have visions...?

An infant in a green mask, puffy.
A cartoon witch riding a broom.
A dead woman, headless.
An apparition.

Incredible nonsense in nothing.

The attempt on the life
Of an ant

Is an act
Which we might compare
To the murder
Of a man.

I have once killed such an insect
And cried,
"Good. You didn't deserve to live."

Listen:

The hum of a bird's coo
The cry of a weaning infant
A rumbling – the earth shattering

Christian McDonough

Say we are looking out a window
And out,
There is a world.

Can we reach this world,
When we are not there?

Not there to watch?
Not there to see?

Between a crack
A light protrudes.

It is there
And brings such lewd
And crude and dangerous

Things to be seen –

Even in such darkness
"A light is seen…"

Life

Did you know! Did you know?
Did you know that it all comes at once?
Did you know that there is no one way?
Everything is changed,
And changes,
At every moment.

Should we say certain words?
Certain phrases and certain things?
If we all said them aloud,
Would we then be more than a crowd?
Would something then begin to change
If altogether we laughed and sang,
"The world has ended and been reborn!
And now another mess is torn.
We are again free, for nothing before
Has meant anything, my friends.
Now together, let us soar."

Infinity lies within a single moment.
An infinity of thoughts, even if from one mind,
All in a single moment.

A lifetime.
Endless lifetimes.

To cut into the flesh
And peel apart the sides;
A red and bloody mess
Which tingles us inside.

The sound of cries and screams
("Ahhhh" or "Ouaaaghh")
As life leaves the victim
And tragedies breed lies.

The scent of rotten things and foul
Odors of hidden nights,
Like semen stained upon the sheets
And blood caked on the walls.

A singeing burn inside the nostrils,
A treacherous leap into sensation –
The purity of action,
Like the straining of a tendon.

We bite into the vicious life
And taste the flesh again,
Renewed with vigor and delight
We burn the past from sin.

Each horror repeats.
Did you know…?
Each horror, again.

I am right here.
I am right here.
You hold me.
You are with me.

Do you see it?
Do you know it?
Is it here?
Is it here?

231

Even in endless suffering
There is overcoming.

Yes,
There is even beauty,
Though it makes me cry.

Why? Why? Why?

“I”
In some great light
And weightless

My face still
And unmoving

Yet “I” am

I am read
And lived

And there is another realm
Where I lay

Eternally

233

Austerity.
Severity.
The world as it is.

Emotions, gone.
Not needed,
Overcome.

"When all is seen
As it must be seen."
For in the face of infinity
We must have calm.

Life is lived a moment at a time,
Though almost all moments are lost and forgotten.
Our lives are given
To endless toil
And we suffer
For the production
Of nonsense.

We must move on from stupidity
And overcome all temptation
So that our indulgence
May flourish
Ripely
And rightly.

We can take it! We can take it!
We don't even have to try!

There are endless moments,
Endless possibilities...

The infinite,
The eternal,
(Yes, it is there!)
And the impossible...

Made true.

You are constantly
Growing...
Growing...

237

Working
Working hard
Doing a job
A shitty job
A dumb job
But a good job
And the job is important
Because it gives you money
And it's not so bad
Though it's shit
And you live
And you live
And you live
Etc.

There are those who speak endlessly...
As if,
Upon ceasing,
They themselves will cease.

Life

239

Your eyes dim on nothing seen
Yet it all stands before you
The world twists and shivers away
And your body seems to leave you
As if your heart had a life of its own
And your soul reached up above
All that rests down below
A bed, a garden, of love

230

People move
Altogether
And let themselves be mindless.

And sometimes
They come to have a mind
Together.

Sometimes they scream at each other
And then again
They are together.

The screams in *here*
Are all together
And in some sense
Will last forever.

We are now in something
That we cannot escape,

And soon enough
Another "break".

And those moments when you were a child
And everything seemed so grand
Horrid how the world was there
And you cut down to the nub
Yet you lived and knew
Because you didn't know a thing
And you could say the truth
And be a wonderfully empty thing

This fantasy here
Is ultimate and true.

Must we speak
All the same

And become
One
Whole
Thing?

The words we feign
Are pale and drained.

Soon enough,

Nothing more
Will reign.

The body collapses in
On itself and washed in mortal sin
You allow the death to be life's way
And are with the trees again
"Scientific! Absolutely terrific!"
And you're a plant in the back seat
As your friends look and see
Your body now, a sack of meat

Life

In the back of your mind
Do you hate those you love?

Everyone
Has desires,
Like to kill
Or to hurt.

And many, many do it.

And many, many scream.

Do you remember
When you last acted
It all out?

Sitting with your infant body
Wading in the sand
Curling your toes
And hugging yourself
Even then

You were a man

247

You and I and we and they
All seem to be thinking things,
But what we do
And what we say

Is forever and ever
Never the same.

Infinite difference,
Yet infinitely similar...

The truth of being,
Of humanity,
Is something
Unfamiliar.

People
Don't like to
Speak much
To each other
Or maybe they would
But it's hard
Because no one seems
To want to
Because everyone is scared
Of what is inside
Of them

Push the muscles
And contract
And push again...

And release,

And God, what a release...!

Such ecstasy
In such moments...
Completely alone,
Oh, yes, completely alone...

For it is the greatest of solitary acts...

Oh, yes, yes...!

Someone behind you
As you sit
And slouch
You hear them
And then again realize
Yourself
And adjust

And they come
And hold you
And you are held

And the moment's passed
But in it
There was something
It must be absurd
Something more
Something beyond
Something *out of this world*

Outside of living
Outside of our reach
Is that where lies
The need for belief?

For those things we can
And cannot know
Are still conceived
Under Earthly shadow...

To pursue
Those great big dreams
You do
Something
You must do it hard
And often
And you'll not get much money
Or any money
But you'll do it
And then come up with
Some reason
Why it is good
And meaningful
To you
And it is
And it really is
But what about
To others?

Flow of thought
May suddenly turn askew

Or

A thousand rivers
Seen all at once

To play with them.
To make them think that you
Are something
When you are nothing.

And something even other
Than that which you believe
Yourself to be:

A thrill
A deception
A fatal mistake...

A cruel and destined mistress
Whom we all must hate.

255

Ignoring others
But you can't
But you can
You need to
But you shouldn't
Because they are there
And you are there too
And without them you're nothing
Maybe not
But less
Because
We seem to die
Without people
Around

To live
Is to be
In such and such a way
To have a way
And follow it.

257

To wish we were in darkness,
To let our bodies waste away.
To become crippled and twisted
Like a rotting tree branch.

This and more
May happen

Yet we go on living.
We breathe a heavy sigh
And pick ourselves up
And move again.

It's a waste.
It's a shame.

And the eyes roll,
And if only we could do it.
Commit that sin.
End the whole thing.

We don't move
We just sit there
And stupid things happen
And we see them
We see them so slowly
In excruciating detail
Mind numbing detail
And then we forget them
And then it happens again

Life

Dreams...
They are perfect escapes
And the worst reality.

They can mean nothing,
Yet shove your face into
All that you *know*.
No matter what you tell yourself,
No matter what you wish for,

And...

They might
Be a chance at
A new self-creation.

You could be that thing,
That headless creature,
Who calls to you
And speaks the truth.

I look and see nothing.
I say nothing.
I know nothing.

But still I speak.
We speak.
We speak and say nothing.

For something.

We sit at the table
And say the words,
The phrases,
That are meant to be said.

And inside
Something stirs,
And purrs,
And growls,
And changes.

Little things crawling on the ground
For their own reasons
Living
Yes, they are
And wonderful
Amazing

Christian McDonough

To change your face
To change your body

To be seen
As something new,
Something different.

"That bug is bugging me."
And the word reveals itself!
A whole world too!
All that there is
In words...
They taunt and trick,
They tickle!

How a word could mean a million different things
And a world is built upon words.

And how
Beneath them
There is something more,
Obscured,
By the word.

The mind slows
To protect itself
Because it believes
It is in danger.
And you have made it
So that each moment
Like this one
Is a threat.

So now you don't move,
You remain still,
While the things around you
Seem to have acute visual detail
Because that is all
Your mind wishes
For you to see.

And you feel "free"
But you are so restrained.
You don't even know
What you cannot obtain.

A fragment of depression
Cuts into your eye
And blinds you.

It hurts.
Or, "it doesn't hurt."

And many love to hide.

But still,
Something,
Empty inside.

267

The airs and winds of vision's mystery come to enshroud us now.
We look into the past again and remember a sullen row...

Wherein we screamed and beat against our head
Saying horrible things,
Such that we'd "be better off dead"
In the face of our life's crumbling.

But in this foggy mist and under this gentle sheath
We do allow ourselves to speak
A sly little squeak...

"How funny,
How crude!
What an absurd way to behave!"

"Oh,
Haha,
It is like this every day."

In isolation we sit
And wonder why we are so alone.

Then we sit with someone else
And again, wonder why we are so alone.

Or,

Why we are in so much pain.

Or,

We live with it, and might like it.

It is dim!
It is dumb!
But there is no real answer!
So we can play
And pretend
All about
Anythin'!
And in between
Beneath the ground
In this "knowing-knowing"...

The smile!
The frown.

Yes.

A master comes and makes with the world...
The Master lives and dies.

Can't we all?

You see,
There are a thousand lives within even me.
An infinity of people that "I" could be.

The body morphs, lengthens, stretches, tears...

Awareness comes! It goes as well.
It grows, at times.

And then,
We reflect back upon them –
Moments.
And see them in a new light.

A true light?
A new light...

And a sensation there...A feeling...

The face will remain unmoved.
"I" will remain unmoved.
"I" am with you.
Do not cower.
Do not fear.
Face it.
And do not worry,
The face will remain unmoved.

Certain points are reached...Processes recur...

You can see the processes of your living, of your thinking,
And then recreate them.

And cause them. New & old...
We must look closely...very closely...

These lifeless things
Given life through our living,
And taken
As though beings.

A teddy bear,
Now a teddy man.
And, by God,
Look at his hands...!

We see them
And throw our own into them,
And what we then see...
Oh, such desires,
Such souls...

There,
In the dead.

Let them come.
Let them live.
Let them bring what they must.

Soon, if you let them,
They will be made

To be

Oh,
So much!

Death will be a comfort.
Well, not really.
But it will be an experience.
An immense experience,
A total experience,
Like me.

Life-like and true:
Your rubber face
Made up like glue.

Each body part a toy
And
A tool

Refigured and reshaped
For whatever new fool

Sees you,
Speaks you,

And you beyond it all...
A beautiful thing,
A tiny little doll.

When we act without thinking,
What are we then?
And when we think?
Are we "not ourselves,"
As some seem to believe?

Yes and yes and yes.
And still "ourselves"
Yet and yet again.

Some sensations
Seem to come,
Yet they cannot be described.

It is a vulnerability
Of the body
That the mind holds it so.

A trickling down
Of vicious reality
Creates what is known

As the ultimate — the untenable — duality,
There shown.

A tragedy made into a farce
When your face falls flat.

You have been through it all,
But now that doesn't mean much.

A life like a veteran's...
An internal fire...

You are the tragedy,
You burn bright and final.

We might try
To say things
And know things
And show things

But there is nothing
That can be shown
Or said
Or made clear

So we speak,
Like those others,
And try,
And try,

But nothing comes.
Only a change within
Can be
Of any
Value,

Can cause
A change
Without.

Everywhere a distraction,
A false process,

For stimulation
And simulation.

These things...
What have they brought?

But grander illusion
And the greatest of delusion.

To reach for something beyond oneself
We look still to others
For they did it first
But there is always someone
Who is truly first
But anyway
We reach
And see
That we have to do those things
That we don't want to do
That we feel we can't do
And then we do them
And so on
And so forth
It's a ladder we must climb
To overcome

We try to overcome
And are often overcome
And then overcome
Etc.

We should try for something completely new
And ridiculous
Shouldn't we?

I don't know
I'm only here
Alive (or dead)
Like the rest of you

All is taken at once
And the running water is heard.

A "truth" is felt,
Never known.

And the ones who speak never seem to say
That which they truly mean.

Should we change ourselves
Again and again?

It might be good.

Have you noticed
The many changes
Within?

Have you noticed what change brings you?
It brings many things...?
But more importantly
It brings new feelings,
Or something like that.

It brings something else
That didn't seem to be there before.
Or else,
It brings the feeling that something new
Is now there.
And perhaps nothing else...

To breathe consciously
Is to choose to live

A triumph
For a moment
Brings something
Or nothing,
Again.

A triumph taken within
Can be bred
And grown
To something beyond
Any "sin."

I don't know
What your life is like.
But I'd like to.
I'd like to hear you speak
About it,
And know it,
And know you.

Alas...

Where are you?
Are you here?

The fantasies we have
Are at times all we have.

And put upon the world
They help us feel

As though something is occurring
Or something is real.

Did you
Think I
Had something
To say?

A thousand moments
Wherein lie
Infinite possibilities
Of experience.

Each
Must be harvested
And plastered
Upon the pages.

Each
Its own,
For itself.

All
Now
A piece
Of something
Greater.

A perfect moment! Split into halves.
From one side seen
As the innocent calf,
Yet from the other
A descent into madness!
None can know,
Nor process,
How it is all only so
Because of those things we suppose ourselves
To know.

Does "I" break away?
Or does it remain?
Can it be
Forever
Contained?

294

Speak aloud
This new phrase,

And all together,

It will be sang,

"Trust me, Trust me,
That this is something,
And when it's something,
It sure ain't nothing!"

Paranoia
And darkness.
When you sit and are vulnerable,
Those shadows
Fill your mind.

When you know
There is something
Behind you
With a knife
Or a cock
To kill you
Or rape you
Or some other fucked terror.

But you still
Know it's nothing
And sit,
Your face blank
And dim
And dumb
And you
Don't know
A thing.

The bones slug off
The skin melts away
The breathing ceases
Today is the day

What is it
That is
Here
Within?

All "I" have seen...
All "I" have known...

And yet, I will return.

No, no, no, no
Don't let him
Whoever he is
Don't let him speak
About himself

I am a child again.
As a man.
A man child.

And this is what we wanted,

And this is what we asked for,

And, by God, this is what we got!

You don't need him
You don't want him
And all that "I" am
Is there
In him?

That place beneath it all
Where visions arise...!
And actions come to be...

Where in darkness
The red mist rises

And movement
Is a virtue.

And...and none of it is there?
All I said was wrong?

Because it cannot be said?
Because it cannot be shown.

It must be lived.
Only then can one say
It was ever known.

I remain
I remain
All that I am
I and not I
And "I" and not "I"

You, me, we, us, and them
A comic tragedy of selves
Who laugh and sing
Lose and wean
Themselves off the teat
Of the bastard
Of the book

303

To trick in play!
To play a game.

To live for competition
Only as a gag.

In the game,
Thank God,

It is then
That there truly are
No rules...!

Bliss! Bliss! Bliss!

Don't let him!
Don't let him!
It will only hurt him!
He doesn't know
He doesn't see
What lies there
In wait
In darkness

<h1 style="text-align:center">295</h1>

Sex and fucking
And coming and jerking
For yourself
Or for the other.

It never really feels good.
There's always something missing.

And there's always more to take.

And it's always so good,

But it never really comes.

And the images in the mind
Might betray
Yourself or the other.

And there's so much work to be done.
Effort is necessary

For anything past the primary.

It takes work.
Hard
Work.

And love
And wetness;

Moisture

And beauty.

A kind of rage
Or sympathy,

And much, much more...

And soon enough
The world will tremble
For all done here
Will Amount!

Life

The past
Doesn't hurt
Anymore

It came back
But it wasn't
Too bad
This time

And the future
Still looks bright
And I'm looking
Ahead

Is that how it is?
Is that all it took?

I forgive him.
I let him.
I can't stand against him.

He is what he is
And he does what he does.
As he must,
As he will.

Haha.
What a thrill.

To lie and deceive;
To deceive yourself
And others.

To cripple yourself
And give a little burden
To all that has anything
To do
With you.

Now,
Go on
And see what lies in store...!

For the horrors
Will be known
And seen,

Desperate
And true,

Cruel
And obscene.

Yet they too will fade.
Haha,
What a stupid charade.

All that he is
In there?

No, no...

Just a taste
Of a nothing.

But whatever,
Farewell!

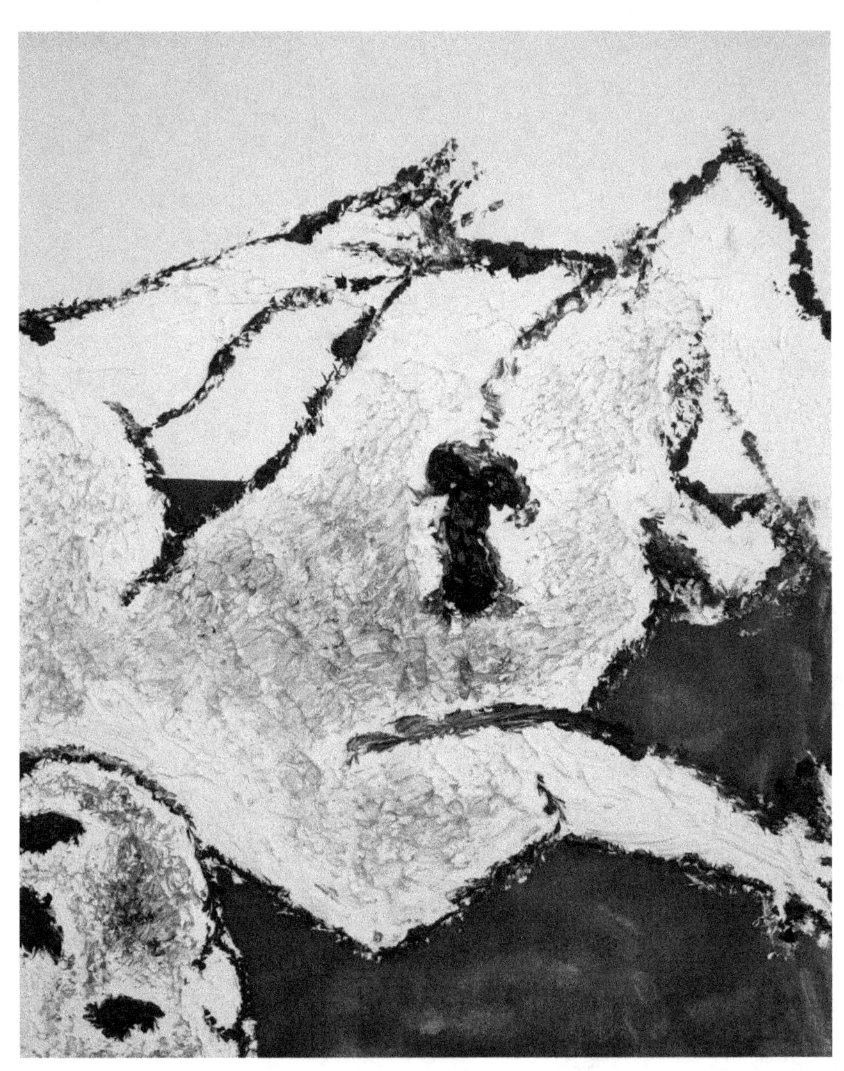

DEAD SOUL

Oh God, Oh fuck
It's me again
The countless hours
I've put into me
In therapy
And thinking
And writing
Oh, writing,
Again!

The bullshit
Of my life
And my stupid
Shit brain

I hate the brain
And other things
You'll learn all about it
Soon,
Soon enough

And my ex-girlfriend
A bitch and a cunt!
I'm not afraid to say it!
I hate her guts!

But I try to forgive
And thank God
I'm moving on

Still she abused me
Or something like that

Who can say
They were abused
When it was all so confusing
And dark
And I was lost

But there are other things too
Things not so depressing
I have parents
And now a great girlfriend

But who knows
How long
Anything
May last

Oh,
How stupid
It's me
What else

316

I remember nothing
As a child
Oh but I remember something
As a child

I liked bugs
And once
I acted as an entomologist
To my family
And discussed them

317

There are times
When
I seem to hate those around me
Those I'm closest to

Well
Some more than others
I want people to respect my boundaries
And have boundaries themselves

I am oh so tired
Of people
Crushing me
With their weight

Once,
"Blaureene",
My ex-girlfriend,
Fucked her best friend
While we were dating
Her best friend, a woman

And still I didn't leave

319

Another time
I cried and cried
Because I thought
Blindia
My current girlfriend
Was going
To murder me

Blaureene
She was manipulative
I think
I get so insecure about this

She was very troubled
And sad
And suicidal
And more

She implied
But almost never said
That if I left her
She'd kill herself

And sex was awful
Maybe something happened to her
But she would often cry
During sex
And she always had me cum
Into a rag

She said cum
Was gross
And icky

And she never seemed to care
How I felt
In sex
Or any other time
Really

I suppose I could try and tell it all now
No need to drag it out
Over a hundred or so poems

She was often mean
She was constantly upset
And when she was upset
She wouldn't move
I really mean it
I mean, not always
But many times
When she was upset
All she would do was lay down
For hours
And not speak
But she was awake

Eventually she did this less

But still
When upset
She wouldn't speak to me

Even when she started moving
And this hurt
Much more
Than you might think
Everything seemed to be
My fault

But it wasn't
But she did blame me
At times

And she would always expect
Me to know
What to do
To fix her
To help her
To listen to her

Though she never told me
Anything

Though I asked
She never obliged

And if I left
When she wasn't moving
Or speaking
She'd immediately text me
That I was weak
Or stupid
Or something like that
And then play the victim
When I tried to defend
Myself

I was with this woman for about five years
And it's true
I'm a sensitive man

But what she did
How she was
Scarred me
Deeply

And visions of her
Patterns of behavior
Thoughts
Feelings
Still recur
When something or other
Reminds me
Of her

321

Now
We can't move on
Because it still haunts me
And I'm sure
I'll have more
Much more
To say about it

I
Am actually
Not
Too sad

Once,
I was younger
And there was a girl
Savannah
Who kissed me
In the room
Of my friend
Who I later learned is gay
But I suppose that's not important
And she humped me
While he was there
And it was a bit odd

I write
And write
And write

And I enjoy writing

Dead Soul

I don't care about people
But also I do
I care deeply
It seems
Though I hate to admit it

I want to live for myself
Not for others

326

I try not to
Look at porn
But still I look at it
And India hates it

Once,
When I was too young
A girl
A bit older than me
Told me she had planned to drug me
And rape me

And I asked
Why she didn't
Just ask!

I love to be stupid
I love to be an idiot
I like not knowing
Sitting there, dim
And saying
"Oh, yes?"

And they tell me
They explain
In great detail
All the things I don't know!
And they feel so happy,
And they feel so proud,

Because now they know
They're the smartest
Of the crowd!

I have a friend
Blaine
Who is very fat
And sad
But good and strong
And strange

I don't care about the world
And the rapes and the murders
And the lies and the corruption
And the bullshit
And oh God the bullshit
That people say

I don't give a shit about it
They just go on and on
And I am here
Alive
On my own!

And I am so thankful
To be happy
And healthy
And living

Oh, thank God
To live and live
All to myself

I work hard
I try
I've had it easy too

So I suppose
You can hate me
For all that

But I don't care!
I'm alive!
I'm living!
And you're not!
Not really!
Haha! Haha!

Oh, no
Do you hate me?

But what does it matter?

I go on and on
Being myself

I wish everyone would be quiet,
For the sake of others
There is too much shit
Around
And it doesn't help
To hear
You dumb fuck bastards
Complain

But no, no
Don't get me wrong
It can be good to complain
It can be important to complain

But some of you
Need to shut your fucking mouths
And sit
And think
And work
On yourselves

Am I showing too much?
Am I too much to take?

No, don't be silly,
I've barely even had
A "hot take!"

I love to sing...
I love to play...

I make all kinds of things,
I do it all day...

And it is well and good,

But sometimes I wonder,

Does it mean anything?
Does it make any difference?

And you, you might say,
"But of course! It's the way
That our culture is formed!
That we change the day!"

But no, I don't believe it.
In fact, I think you're dumb.

I know it's all stupid
And that's what makes it so fun

I like women
That look like young boys

Oh, that sounds weird,

Well, anyways,

I like them a bit manly,
But girly, too.
Sometimes I wish I liked men
But only a woman will do.

Sometimes sex seems mostly ugly and difficult
And uncomfortable
And bad

And sometimes I love it
And am very happy to do it
And think it's wonderful

I'm not sure why it's like this for me
I thought it was because of Blaureene before
And she certainly made it much much worse

But even before
There was a lot of anxiety
And fear

With sex

I suppose
Something could have happened
That I don't remember

But I don't know

Anyway

321

Really I just want everyone
To want to fuck me
And to love me
And to think I'm a darling cutie pie
A sweetie
With good looks

"And he doesn't even know it!"

And everyone to praise me
And say I'm a good boy
And pat me on the head
While inside I devour them
And sexualize them
And kill them
Because I am oh so much better than them
And oh so much more thoughtful
And talented
And naturally so
Because it's just who I am
Oh so wonderful
And sweet
And thoughtful
And cool
A little baby
For everyone
To love

Oh god
I'm so gross
And disgusting

And I love it
I love it
I love it
I love it

I'm a man
With a big cock
And a big appetite

And I hate it
I hate it
I hate it
I hate it

Disgusting scum fuck
That's me
Don't give a damn
Pee behind a tree

And I'm free
Free
Free
Free

I like watching movies
And visiting other worlds

I like being a baby
Not a little girl

I spend time doing nothing
Watching dumb things

Or beautiful genius perfect things

And I love some things
And hate some too

I'm already gone
From this world
It's true

I don't care
If my rhymes
Are poor

I write for myself
For me
Not for you

I write so that something
Might happen to me
Maybe I could learn something
Or change again
And be free

I remember when I was young
I didn't like it
When I had socks on
And they constricted the movement
Of my toes

So once
I had my mom
Cut holes in them

And I remember when I was young
I was so very shy
And I remember looking at girls
And wishing
They were mine

Sometimes I'd sit
In the same way as them
So they might notice
When looking
That I'm just like them

And sometimes I remember
Walking through the school halls
In line all together
And thinking in my head
Of all I might say
To a girl
Or to someone
Or to an imaginary creature
And I might make the faces
And might mumble
Or mouth
The words
That I'd say
If I could have spoke

And I remember being embarrassed
Because I didn't realize I was doing it
And someone looked at me
And made a face

Christian McDonough

I don't need to live
I think when I die

Maybe the things
That I write
Will come with me
And help me
To see

And show me
The things
They were truly meant to be

Because I've heard people say
That in death they see
All kinds of funny things

Like god in a tree
And great big visions
Of meaningful landscapes
Without concrete shape
Without form or place

And the thoughts
The ideas
Aren't they there too?

Maybe I'll go
And bring my own with me too

Hahahahahaha!
I'm really quite happy!
I'm a happy person!
Oh yay!

But sometimes I lay
And wonder
If I'll ever amount
To anything

And all the things I do
Are they meaningless
To me?

Or just meaningless
To everyone else?

I don't know
I don't know

Am I failing myself?
Should I be doing something else?

It doesn't matter
At least I'm doing
This

328

I should kill myself
Aw jeez
I lay around
And stay in bed
And do nothing
And waste away

But later I'll get up
And do something
And feel fine

329

Me, me, me, me, me, me
Me me me me me
I love being myself
And not doing much
Sometimes people really love me
And like how I am
Sometimes I get very irritable
And annoying
And a bit rude

You don't know me
But I guess not many really do
There's so much that I don't say
Even to those I'm close to
It's hard to say things
There are many things I don't know how to say
Not that they're hard to say emotionally
Or anything like that
It's just hard sometimes to even think to say some things
When they're so much in your thoughts
Not in your world
And then
If I were to try to say them
It feels as though they can't really be said
Or when I say it
It's not saying what I thought
Or what I want
And the other doesn't understand

I could do anything I want here
It's me
It's mine
It's all for me
Haha

Those nights
Where,
By my own ingestion,
The world split into two
And I dragged about the floor
As if I were
A great, unwieldy beast,
A creature,
Destroying all in my sight.
And I might have died...
I thought I died...
But stupidly,
I lived!

It's important to me
That the people I'm with
Are nice
And strong
And thoughtful

Well
Not completely

I like some people
Who seem happy
Just to be
And don't worry too much
About anything
Or at least
That's how they make it seem

I like people
Who have strong opinions
Too

They are fun
To listen
To

But sometimes I get annoyed
As I'm sure you know
And sometimes I
Have opinions too

I used to think
I'd be this or that
But it keeps on changing

It's hard to know
What to do
For money

Something meaningful
Is nice
But it takes a lot
Of money
Then
To make it

Haha
Haha

I like to laugh
I didn't think I was funny
But maybe I am

333

That man,
Really, that boy…
Amazing how easy it had been
To manipulate the little me.
And his hate, so charismatic,
And it fell upon me.
The truth is never simple.
My life was never free.

All that he gave me,
And all that I took…
We walked upon a path
That fateful night,

And a fork arose,
And I laughed and laughed.
And that was the night
That I stayed,
That that woman,
Was "mine."

Father, forgive me.

348

Philosophy
Has meant
So much
To me

Dead Soul

You wouldn't believe
How much of a horror
I was
I beat my best friend
And helped him with his wish to die

And still,
Years later,

We returned
And have together
Cried.

Oh
I'm not much
Of a person
Not really

I'm a little bitty leaf
In the wind
With a shape
And some veins
And a color

But not much else

I could be many other things

God
It's so hard

I want to write
Meaningless things
That then become meaningful
Incidentally
Haha

Things that speak to people
Somehow
Just because
And that's it

She always put me in the wrong
She was never happy
She was always upset with me
I constantly tried to break up with her
For the last few years
But she wouldn't leave me alone
Even if I blocked her
She'd find some other way to contact me
And she even tried to keep me from my family
And she seemed to have no thought for my feelings
For she said
That my feelings made it so
That she wasn't allowed
To feel a thing
And I believed everything she said
For a long time
Perhaps that was the worst of it
And for a long time
I was alone
For years
Alone
With only her
By her own hand
Nothing was ever enough

I used to care
About analyzing myself
And uncovering my hidden drives
And desires
But now
I don't really
Give a shit

I've done that work
For a while
And now it's time
Just to live
And be
As I am

I don't care!
I don't care about the self!
I don't care about the psyche!

I suppose I'm at an impasse
And a change is occurring
And soon I'll find
Something new
To care for

I get so sad
When my thoughts
About my girlfriend
Get confused
With thoughts
About my ex-girlfriend

And I don't know
Whose face is who
For a moment
Or two

I hope
Some strangers
Will read this book
And reach out to me
To speak with me
And I
To them

I like to paint
And make music
And make films
And to read
And to write

Hahahahahahah
It's so funny
That I'm doing this
Right now
And it's here

I want to be able
To say things
That are meaningful
And can connect me
With something else
Something greater than me

I want to reach
Some great place
That is divine
And mystical

And to see
Things
That have never before been seen

And to speak
Things
That have never before been spoken

I want to experience it
Feel it
Know it
And hold it

I want it all
Again
And again
And again

I love being a man!
Oh…!
I'm so big and strong!
I have a huge dong!

To my best friend
I was a bastard
And an old best friend
Had been a bastard to me
I suppose it's fate
That we are filled with hate

I bullied my best friend
And my old best friend
Fucked my ex-girlfriend

And everyone
Was oh so sad

My best friend,
My old best friend,
And my ex-girlfriend

Oh, woe is me!
To be surrounded
Desperately
With the saddest sacks
All about town

Drowning and drowning
In their salty tears
While I fiddled with myself
And wasted a few years

I am the king of masturbators
I stimulate myself
So supremely
That anyone who might see me
Would think surely
To deceive me

For...

"He doesn't deserve it!
No man should be
So happy
So pleased
Alone
With only
Himself!"

Whenever I found out
That she and him
Got together
It was maybe less than a month
After she stopped talking to me
(Imagine! She finally stopped! But I was so fucked and desperate by that
        point I didn't know what to think.)
And a week or two
After I started talking to him
Again
And I was distraught
And cried and screamed
And it was very embarrassing
I felt the only two people I had put my trust into in my life
Had intentionally betrayed me
And I couldn't sleep
And I remember
It was horrible
I called him
And asked for all kinds of details
And I cried to him
As if he could comfort me

I should have died

348

I don't know anything
At all
About myself

I am lost
I am dazed
When I wonder
Who I am

I am a figment
A loss
An empty and abstract
Thing

I don't know
What to do
I don't know
What I am

I try
For something
And that could be me

I've lost myself
I've made myself
Free

And there was another time
When trying to leave her behind
I even warned her
I even asked her directly if I could
A terrible triangle
A disgusting creation
Emerged
And exploded

I remember
For a time
I was really
Very stupid

I looked deep
Into things
And thought that I
Was seeing something more

This might sound quite heroic
And warranted
And worthy

But you weren't there
You don't know
What it was

You see I
Heard simple phrases
In books and films
And thought that they
Were obscure
Intentional
Purposeful points
Toward a whole other meaning
Beyond common sense

And not only that
But the true meaning of them
The typical meaning
What they actually said
Was lost on me
And confused
For I couldn't see things
As they were seen
By the others
All around me

This was at a time
When I was quite low

The things I did
And the people around me
Were not good for me
And hurt me dearly
Perhaps I was lost
In pain and suffering
And turned towards confusion
As a kind of buffering

To save myself
To help myself
I made myself stupid
And fell deep inside
And then I returned
And, by God,
Something has survived

I am so glad
That I don't
Prostrate myself
Before you cunts
And tell you
How things must be
How things are wrong
How people must behave this way
Or that way
Because it is good
And right

That I don't beg you
For your approval
By telling you
About the ills of the world
And giving examples
Of ugly
Bad people
And their
Poor behaviors

I am not a fucking dumbass!
I am not a worthless piece of shit!
I am myself!
With my own thoughts!
And my own beliefs!
That I can keep
To myself…!

Heheheheheh
Hahahahahaah
Ohhh
Well
Maybe not
Maybe so
I guess I really
Just don't know

353

I might pray to a God
Whom I create
And call her
The Great Androgyne

And she lives to un-fuck
To un-cum
To suck dry
And unbirth

I wish I could escape
From all the horrible distractions
And pressures
That I don't need
And everyone else
Seems to love

Christian McDonough

I like looking
At sexy women
All the time
All the time

No matter what anyone says

I'll fucking kill you
I'll fucking kill you
I'll fucking kill you
I'll fucking kill you

I won't put anyone else's poems here
Not friends nor family

It's all for me
It's mine
Only mine
Only me

I want to hurt people
Just a little

And show them something
Rub their face in it all

Sometimes
I have so much anger
And hate
In my heart

And I want you to know it
I want you to see it

I will not give it up
Not for you

And when I can finally show my hate
It dissipates,
Fades away,
And I can again care
For everyone
And everything

Oh,
I'm so happy,
I'm so free

358

And there was the time
When I tried to run away
From a good love
And many times
Of confusion
And terror
Some odd primal fear
That I couldn't truly process
Or understand
It just struck me
And I couldn't calm myself
And I felt as though I were
In the past
With her
Again
I suppose that's the real trouble
It confused me
So much
And I couldn't know
What was right
Or wrong
What was in my head
Or there
True
And real

I didn't know
I didn't know

All because of her
All because of her?

All that I am
Could already be here
But I also want to be
All that I am not

Sometimes I feel
Like I'm just a body
And there's just the tingle
Of being alive

And I'm just a machine
Trapped into
This world
That I can't escape

Dead Soul

375

I had a dream last night
That I saw Blaureene again
And we almost had sex
But I remembered that
I was with India
And told Blaureene
That I didn't want to see her
And that I had to go
And I left

Oh, yes
I can play with myself
And pretend to think
Deeply
About who I am
And all my desires...
And all those things
Hidden within me...

All I do is for myself...
I used to volunteer...
Oh, yes, to help others,
I used to work in mental health
Oh, so selfless...

But I also did it
To make myself feel better
To improve myself
To have a chance at certain graduate
     programs
Etc.

My god! Everything! Selfish!

Yes, wow, what a great thought.

And, oh...
Why did I let myself
Stay in that horrible relationship
For so long...?

Because! I didn't feel I deserved any
     better...
Oh...! I deserved to suffer!
I wasn't good enough for anything
     more!

Yes...! Yes...!

And...why should I tell you these
things...?

For attention!
For sympathy!
For pity!

So that I can look at myself and say,
"Oh...... I tried my best...
"I'm just a baby......
"I just can't do any better......"

And escape any real responsibility
Oh, yes...
Such truth!
Such self-understanding!

Wow, wow, wow

Bon Appétit!

Dead Soul

Shame, shame, shame
Much of my life was lived in shame

I will not let you shame me

Shame against sex
Shame against speaking
Shame against thinking

I don't know where I found it
But it was with me for years

I hated myself
I hated my desires

I hated those that would speak
With confidence
Without forethought

Because I knew
What they could do
I could not

But I won't let you shame me
No, not again
I won't let it repeat
Or worsen
Like it did with Blaureene

I will be completely disgusting
And revel in it too
I will destroy good taste
I will destroy you

I don't need to do
All that I say I'll do
I used to care about being honest
Now I think anything will do

I'm crumbling
I'm fading
I'm already gone
You don't need to miss me

I'm off to the beyond

No
I don't want to lie
I don't want to not care
I want to have principals
Beliefs
Yet again!

I want to ask things of people
And have high standards
And tell them to shove off
If I feel they don't meet them

But also
For those others
Who are not close to me
I'd like to be
Some benign
Yet positive
Presence

A comfort

People often tell me
I am a comfort

You know
I don't want to talk about me
I want to be here for you
For a little bit at least
And comfort you

What do you do?
What do you like?
Do you sit quietly at night
And wonder when
Someone will come along
To hold your hand?
To help you out?

Well, here you go
I'm here, right now.

I know you're sad
I know you're angry
But come and hold me

I'll be a mother to you
Or a father
(For those sad, lonely ladies...)

And I'll ask you things
And tell you things
And everything
Will change.

Dead Soul

Oh...
Us together!
It is so nice
Not to be alone!

I can tell you my story!
And perhaps it will relate to yours...

We will be together
Forever
Within these words.

368

Oh, yes
I can understand
How a woman could hate a man

I too have the desire
To withhold sex
And use it as a weapon

To remain silent
And build a sense
Of oppression

To complain and complain
And let the other remain
In doubt
And in shame

But I don't do it!
Because I know it is wrong!
Because I know it hurts!

Did she know it?
Dumb old Blaureene?

Well, it doesn't matter,
Does it?

Now it is foreign.

Oh,
I just thought of this
Maybe
Because of the trauma
I have severed
A part of myself
That is very nice
And gentle
And beautiful

Maybe

I could get it back
Or let it
Return

Oh,
Will everyone hate me?
Will everyone think I'm a liar?

I suppose some things point against me
And in this day and age
That's all it might take
To throw me away

Oh, well
Whatever,
I say what I say

And at least I can say that I said it

I really want to convey
How it was
With Blaureene
It's hard to say it
For a while
It was hard to remember much
With her it felt almost constantly bad
If I disagreed with anything she said
She would get very upset
And shut down
So I could never discuss anything
       with her

And
I don't know
I don't think she ever cared about me
When she got with Blakley
My old best friend
He mentioned to me
(Because I for some reason continued
To be his friend
For a time)
Some very personal things she told him
Though she had never told me
Anything of the kind

And I should mention too
That Blakley
Was a bastard
Very rude
And much more hateful
Than I

Blaureene
Had previously
Pushed me
To stop being his friend
Because of how hateful he was
(Or so she said)

How funny then
That she'd then go
And fuck him
After I stopped being
His friend

(He later reached out to me
Just before or maybe just after
He started fucking
Blaureene.
Soon enough,
I was told)

I should also mention
That Blaureene
Tried to blisolate me
From other friends too
Though I only ever had
A few

Why is it so important to me
That I show
That she abused me

Why do I care so much
About others perception
Of that situation

Because maybe
For so long
I never knew
Whether I was right
Or wrong

Because with her
Everything became
Completely muddied
And I felt as though I had
No will of my own

Except in my art
Except in my writing

There is something very enticing about the idea of upsetting people
I could get so much attention
And people would think about me

Oh no

When I was a few years old
I took out my penis
And said to my grandma
"You ever seen one of these?"

When I was in pre-school
Apparently
My teacher had to tell me
To keep my lips
To myself

I remember
I used to want to be
A scientist
And do all kinds of strange
Experiments

One that my uncle remembered
Was that I put
A rubber band
In a bowl of water
And froze it
To see what would happen

I imagine
That the kind of experiments
I really wanted to do
Involved colorful chemicals
And beakers
And my hair growing long and white
And remaining up spiked

I wanted
To create
Something
I think

When I was young
I wanted to make video games
But I wanted them to mostly be stories
With lots of cutscenes

And I wanted to be immersed deeply in the games I played
I imagined there would be complex worlds
Within them
And strange characters
And it would feel
Like so much
So much

I loved Crash Bandicoot
Especially

I think I wrote out
A story once
And drew a character

About a somewhat cat-like
Humanoid creature
With a dragon
Made of turds
(A chain link of turds)
Coming out
Of his ass

(Again, I was very young)

The first girl
That I can remember
Showing an interest in me
Had short, boyish hair
And seemed like
A tomboy

She was very nice

I, I, I...
Oh, me,
And all I am...

I sing...
I dance...
I play...

I love myself
I love myself

(I hate myself)

A great man
A horrible bastard

(God's Little Bastard)

I could overcome.
I could become.

I traverse the planes
Of my possible selves

And produce
Such beauties
As this

I am a man
A woman
A child

I don't know, I don't know

I am Christian McDonough

I speak my name

And live my life

I won't let this
Be taken from me

Haha, haha

Yes, "this,"
Is mine.

382

Wild nights
Of my past

In *this* moment
I can look upon them happily
And revel in them

But I really only see them
As a dark shade
Upon my life

No...?

I imagine
They have given me much
Yes, how I am
How I behave

Much of this
Is to do with
My many nights
Of weariness
And derangement

Oh,
Such golden
Ever-laden
Nights

About the world
I walked
Surrounded
By fools
Like myself

Yet not
No,
Who was I?

And what were they
To me?

They took me
He took me

I had almost forgotten

He pushed me
To be
Something
Like him

How strange
Now that I know
Just how weak
He had been

I had a dream
Where he
Was a child
Abandoned
And I
Took pity
And helped

I had a dream
Where she
Had not left

And I cried
And screamed

But couldn't
Escape

I remember my old neighborhood
The one I grew up in

Oh and that girl
The one who took me to the forest
When I was younger
And she a bit older...

But I remember
That oval
The houses aligned
Surrounded by forest

It was simply divine

Me,
A young child
So sensitive and shy
Surrounded by greatness
To one with green eyes

Ahhh,
Such peace
In my anxiety

When I look back and see
The young, little me

I suppose
I think
Deep down
That I'm dumb
And that
Makes me feel
Very bad

But I think
I could be
Getting past it

I should be

If I haven't
Already

But it could be
Pretty deep
Within me

So
Who knows

I remember crying
In my old therapist's office
About this

It's hard
To remember
Your problems

I have been journaling for years
About myself
Sometimes it helps
Sometimes I don't put much effort in

Sometimes I get anxious or upset
And I write in it
And I think I feel a bit better

Christian McDonough

I know. I know.
I'm sure it was my fault too.
I should have left.
I should have tried harder.
But I wasn't able to.
And I'm sure I was shitty.
I got so upset.
She always acted
Like it was all my fault.
So, I'll forgive her.
I'll forgive him too.
If only so
I can move on.
And forget.

I think
My earliest memory
Is of me
Crawling under the dinner table
At my parents' old house

And looking up
To see
People's lower halves

I remember
Once
I cried
Because my lips
Were chapped
And my father
Brought me chapstick
And took me home
From school

392

I remember my father
Had a character
That he would become
Called Simbian
Some kind of
Ape man
Who loved us
And carried us
And threw us
Into the pool

I remember my mother
Would pretend
That she was
Hannibal Lecter
And do the mouth thing
And tell us
How she'd love to eat our livers
With a nice bottle
Of Chianti
As she tickled us
And we laughed

I remember my Grandmother's arm
And hand
Would become
A tiny woman
Named Bitsy
With a headscarf
And lipstick

Bitsy spoke
In a high voice
And I think
Scared my sister

Dead Soul

I remember
My sister
Used to "hug" me
But actually
Squeeze me
Too tightly
And I would cry

I remember also
My sister
Would walk towards me
With cute bunny sunglasses
And I would cry
Horrified

411

And also I was told
That my sister
Wouldn't allow
Others to come near me
Because I
Was much
Too
Precious

I remember my younger brothers
Growing up
And they still grow now
And it is so beautiful
To see them change
And become
What they are

And I remember myself
Again and again
And all that I am
And all that I have been
And all that I will be

And I let it go
And let it return
And I look and see
Whatever there is
Whatever will be

Haha
Hahahaha
Now!
To throw away my silly self!
And to see what lies in store
When I am nothing!
When I am gone!
Away!
Away with me!
Now to the heights
To the uplands
Of absurdity!

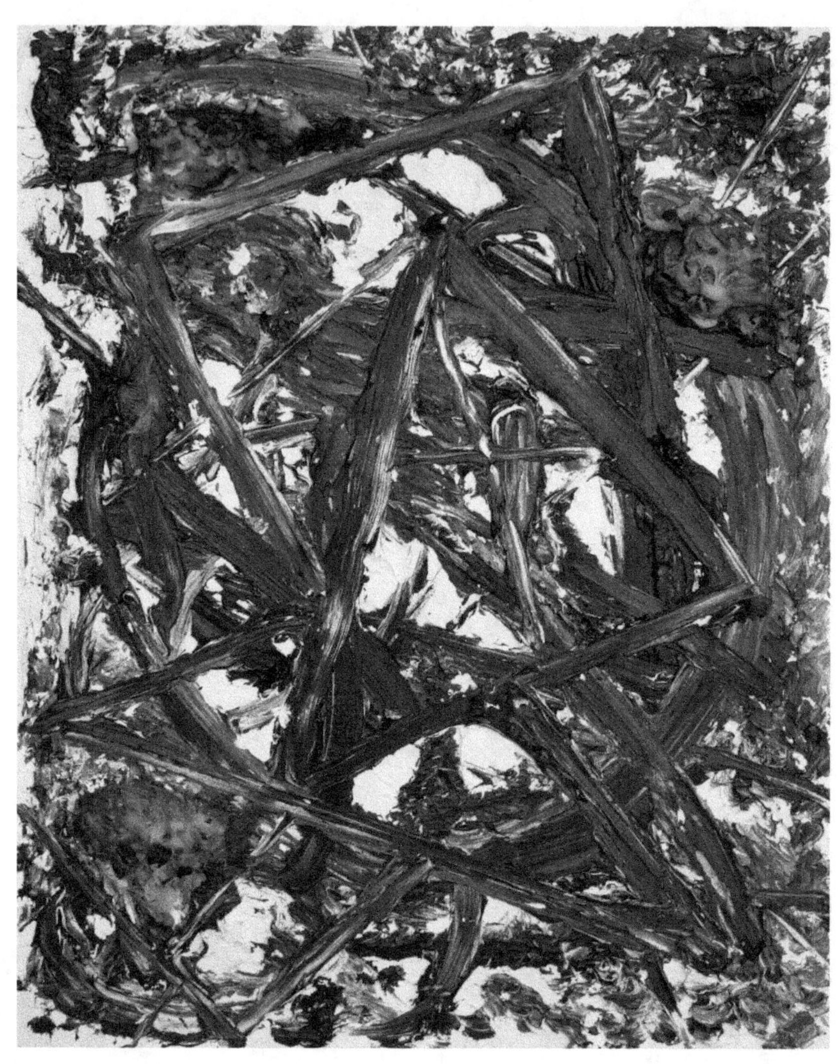

UPLANDS

Everything fading away...
Ohhh... And
Returning
Reviving
Ohhhh...!

Oh, absurdity, absurdity, absurdity...

I cannot
I cannot stop.

It goes and goes
On and on
And
Oh shit
And
Oh fuck
And

402

The doom stopper is stopping you!
He is coming.
It is coming
For you!

And the plants are here
Yes, the plants are here

They are here for you to know.
For you to show
What it is that you
Might be
In that space,
That dome,
That domestic capacity
Of living.

And being,

You know
In the way
That plants be,

As they be and be,

Etc.

Again, again
Hate.
Hate for me,

For they see me
And know me

In all the men
That they might be.

I cannot accept.
No, I cannot accept
Any
Any
Any

Of this.

For without
And within
There is
A great sin.

I am nothing
I am empty
I am the drained balls
Of the sea...

And I do not see
Any
Thing
Within me

Which is clean.

The great devil
Has now come
For your cunt
(Or maybe cock or anus)
(We can't say for sure)

And now you must
Do
What is necessary.

You know what it is,
Don't you?

A little yellowtail
Blessed his mother
With the hail.
And upon her head
A beating
Dead.

And he then called himself Withnail.

A miserable mist,
A terrible twist.
A disgusting malfunction,
A cantankerous *contruption*.

This, that, and the other

Which is and is not...

Yes, this simple model
From which these pages are wrought.

No, do not know,
Nor speak, nor say,

For I am a liar
And you are my prey.

How beautiful,
To be lost
And to find
It again.

I am crushed.
I am blunted.
I am beyond the past,
My friend.

I, a baby,
Live to know
What lies in store

On the great shores
Of the intelligence
And the irrelevance

Of the creation of new modes
And new forms
Of malevolence.

Yes,
Ahh...
It feels good
To be a babe.

For I am so young,
So weak
And misbehaved

That I don't really have a worry
But I can allow myself to think

While I hold out my glass
And have another sip
From my mother's teat.

Unencumbered,
Unbinblundered,

A false flag of the faggots.

This is too much,
Much too much.

Chum oot Chum,
Give them some

And make them all the more.

I do not hate them.
I do not bait them!

I simply knock upon the door.

I might end up rewriting
Everything for which I've been fighting
And remaking my something
Into another feared nothing,

For I do not know
What is good,
Nor what glows...

For within,
A burning
Yearning
Happens for that thing

Which
Is everything
And all
And kindling...

Oh, ho.
What a worry,
What a wondering.

I frowned and cried,
I nearly died!

I was a forest
And a tree.

I was a mouse
With fleas.

I wished for less,
For no one,
For nothing.

But all I got
Was this stupid old

"Something."

413

Trials and failures
And trapped measures
And men's mires.

These things,
These possibilities,
Should they concern
Us writers?

Oh, God.
Who are you?
And what do you write?

Another, another,
And others, and others,

I don't know,
I don't know,

But again and again

I become what I wanted,
I become what I am.

In training,
In trying,
I find horrors abound.

I am not a coward!
I did not attend Brown.

Is the mystery
Of my misery

Here,
In the hound?

I held his round face
And petted him down,

But still he jumped up
And barked at me!

"Oh, Hun,
Do not do this.
I do not find it fun."

You cannot stop me from continuing my stupidity and my life. It is
    unforgivable and unthinkable!
You don't
Even know
It.

The shit birds go on... My, my...

A wish
A wonder
A wild
Stinking
Blunder.

The female form
Is of the
Flying tiger.

So strong
So vicious
So viperous
And voluminous.

I don't really care
To go on
And on like this.

Your rules mean nothing;
The riots are coming.

The blacks and the browns,
The yellows and the crowns

Are raising their glasses
And finalizing their taxes,

For the fires of the furnace
Are blazing in Texas.

A tragic horse manure mover treated
The youth banger fry
(That little munchkin one there)

As a kind of
Horror

(Not unlike a film)

And unmade
All
That it was.

Ah
Lord,
A shame that it is me,

For you people do not know
What this will soon mean.

The heatdeath of the world
Is sure to be here soon

And your mother, your father,
Your crumbling born,

Are soon to know
What was meant...

When it was said, "Forlorn..."

All I wished for,
Fallen away.

And now
Nothing.

Nothing.

Nothing

Remains.

A shy vial
Of the ultimate cream,

Wherefore without
The blight is be-dreamed...
A wallow,
A widow,
A wide-bearing load!

The loaf of ignorance...
The mild cold.

I tremble,
I totter,
I teeter and say,

"No.
I didn't do it.
Not on this day…"

423

Untethered to life,
And broken away from misery...
I now can wonder
What it is
That is in me

Again.
Again?

No, not again.

From the beginning.
From the end.

We will look at the past,
At the previous,
At the last –

Oh. You see,
I say many things
To myself and to others...

To be,
I must tell you,
I *pretend*.

442

No, no, no
Nothing.

A pot of ham.

A steam of something.

443

This all will come
Soon enough
Or later,

And when you get there
Tell your mother (or father)
You'll see her (or him) later.
Much later,
Much later,

For you won't need the past.
You won't need the birth,
You won't need that mast.

A life is lived
And a baby is born.
A new one is coming
And "I" is unlearned.

The creature looks with downcast eyes
And wonders, wonders, to his own surprise,
"What will it be, in the end, with it all?
Will he be arisen, renewed, enthralled?"

It all returns
To me & you.

Every figment,
Every fragment...

A piece,
A puzzle

Of us,
Of our

World
Which we birth
And raise...

Oh, God.
I love you.
We play.

A triangle
Forms the bond of Green

Within the bi-flected angle
Of the drought
(OF 1847)

Which brought such sorrow

To that dying town
(IN WROCLAW)

And begun the benign
Buffering
Of
The
Sheen.

A train bursts through my heart
And into yours.
And we
And us
Again
Are free.
A lover,
A fighter...

You are everything
To me.

I became a bastard for you, mama.
I took down the tasks for you, mama.

I did
Only what I had to do...
Mama...
It's true...

I measured it like a spoon, mama.
I feathered it like a bassoon, mama.

Oh, all,
Oh, everything...

Mama.

The banquet!
It is awaiting!

Where we
Shall dance!

A performance
Must be given
And the rites
Must be spoken.

Y sprach!
Que?! La amore!
Tiende *Mien* Natura
O, czym?

A flower is petaled.
It breaks
A word

And allows one to contour
Upon the world.

A choice,
A chance,
A wish
In that glance,

As each petal picked
Begins the dance.

A flagrant fingering of the asshole
In the mass hall
With the priest there
And the deceased care!

434

A wire
We hang on

Upon each day's beginning.

A mother,
A father,

For each step of winning.

The tidal wave comes in
And the wilds reach in,

And a misty parade
Longs
For the end of the coming day.

Oh, sweet chariot,
Whereupon rides my bliss...

Come back again
When I have to take a piss.

The reaping has been done.
The song still remains unsung.

The words now must be spoken.
All must be said aloud.

And then

The Life may arise
And Become.

The meaning,
The knowledge

May be, perhaps,
Known
And created

As it was destined to be.

Yes,
For there is something
Beyond this,

Something great.

> A WORLD ARISEN
> A DEATH TOLD
> A RIDDLE HELD
> A MESSAGE BORN

Flies buzzing
About the (mostly) fresh corpse,
Tending to our Earth,
To nature's general girth.

The beginning and refitting
Of this
Into that.

LIFE!

How our world
Loves it.

OH, LIFE.

Yes, life.

I hate it.
I hate you.

And all
That it
Contains
And remains
As

I'm sorry, no
Not you...

OH! OHHH!

It
Is
Is
Is...

THE BLACKNESS SUBSUMES
THE CCCCCREATIONNNN
OF AN ACCOMPLICE! A LIE!

I do not know why.

But if you
Were a parent

(Maybe specifically
A mother)

You might think
That your own father
Was a bastard?!

IMAGINE THAT!

Become that...
Which you need...
For your own...

LIFE!

LIFE!

457

Little girls and little boys
Play, play, play with their toys.

Oh, ouch.
(Now me a gentle liberal)
How they are rough,
Much too rough,
When they toddle and tinkle.

Ah
Acka
Allah

Haha

Bum
Numb

Begin
Anew
And uncover
Unconquered
My shoe
My shoe

Strident, pure.
(Now me a cruel conqueror)
A dire serving
Of the brains of the poole.

You there, come hither,
And take me by the tool.

I crush you,
I flush you,
Down with my stool.

Sayonara,
Old chum...
With your big belly-tum!
You blasted the brains
All across the begaine

And grew and grained
The Trial of Stain.

Straighten out,
Straighten up,
Trollop and chew
Your own soul up silly
And become a fool.

444

There is nothing to stop me,
Nothing to hold me back,
Nothing to make me,
Nothing to wrack.

A thousand insects
Crawl upon my body.

The flesh, the flesh tingles
And the insect legs squirm.
I do not like it!
I do not like it!

Oh, God! It burns!

Empty, empty, empty

Oh,
And the eyes,
They look at me
And I see them as if my own
And their faces,
Hard,
Shelled,
Blown-up
To eat me,
And their maws
Open
And everything within,

And suddenly
My penis is severed
And I am so alone
And empty
And drained.

I'm being drained!
Drained!

Can't you see what it's like??
It's absolutely insane!

Woosh
Waash
Across the great sea,

Come be a pirate
And swindle with me.

I again
I again

So much pain
An itching

But the trial remains
Oh...
Oh God...

For a moment I felt it

Yes, what was there...

I felt it
And what it is becoming

God, I'm so happy
I'm so happy

You don't know
You simply don't know

How happy I am

Oh, what a shame that you can't experience
What I experience
That you can never know it
As I have known it

Oh, God,
Such freedom
Such wonderful
Playful
Bliss

This, that, and the other... Soon again, I'll be made of rubber.
If you are wise, you'll wish it too. Upon yourself, become a tool.
I only warn you for feeling, as I have more than none.
And I am a sailor, from here to that nun.
I-I-I and I
You, see, I, and be
For this or for that
For some or for none

Again and again, the bundle undone.

448

I could interrupt everything now and say something to you directly.
I am happy that I have this freedom, but what to do with it all?
I don't know what it is. I don't know what is there.
But something is coming. Can you feel it? Do you dare?

I wish for the powers
Of great, precarious mimes
(or minds)
To overtake me
And wash away my blindness
And give me a clean slate
For about twenty minutes.

A ball cannot drop
Without a good cough.

451

An infinity in fucks.
Oh, yes,
A return
To the way that it once was.

Could I never give up
On all that I have been?

Oh, a failure,
Yes,
A failure.

A decapitation
Of the spitroast
Of the spitfuck

Forever...!

The riots are won
When blindmen are done,

And killers are caught
Where werewolves are not.

Whistle to me
About the long
And dreary dreams
Where your life is lived
For hours, days, years!

And when you wake
You see
Not a moment
Has passed.

It has all gone by
In nothing!
A flash!

Uplands

I wish I could kill
A million things,

But it is unknown
What is here
And what remains.

The time passes
And portends
Its night
As the brawlers continue
Their everlong fight.

It is so weary
How it doth glow...
And the growth, the growth,
It goes by
So slow.

1 and 2 and 3 and 4,
I called your mother
A dirty whore.

5 and 6 and 7 and 8,
I was just kidding
You know she's great.

I reach deep within
And take out
From the pit

An endless,
Tragic,
Flagrant
Bliss.

And it shows me
And gives me

All that I am,

And it takes me
And controls me

To the end
Of *the man.*

Minstrels of meat
And masters who cheat,

These things are one and the same.
Oh my!

477

If only...If only...
You knew the day

Would come
And become

Upon the neigh,

Where the beasts,
Oh, the beasts,

Shall rise up!
And say!

That (Harumph!)
"This day is that day!"

The blind bats fly.
The creepers cry.

For, oh, such misery...
To be such a small fry.

Live and live and live again.
I know you want it,
You want it to end.

But life goes on
Whether we want it or not,

Even beyond
The total death of our lot.

The...Delicacy...
(This is a song)
Of...Matriculating...
Of...That most obscene...!

Oh...I love...Money...!

I need...To be...
Hungry...!

To do – to do – All that I need –
To do – to do!

How, How, How...!
It's's's's you!

The Deceiver...
The Receiver...

That which belongs!
That which revolves!

Oh, don't worry...
Don't trouble ye...

It is
Like a mother

With a brother
Suckling
Suckli-i-i-ng
The milk
From the
Teat!

Oh!
What a feat!

To be simply
Sweet!

So sweet!
So sweet!
So sweet!
So sweet!

Yes, all will die –
This planet, I mean.
But still a new world
Will soon be seen.
To have life,
To live life,
To be and have been.

For we cannot forget
The infinite
Of the unseen.

That thing you did that one time was something that I didn't like.
Yes, I'm not afraid to say it! I have done it and now it is done!
You have been confronted! Confronted forever! And
YOU CANNOT ESCAPE IT!

The trials we face
And the trails we take
All lead to nothing.

But still there is something...

For in each choice
An infinity arises

And we must make
The most of our prizes,

For laughter is sweet
And birds go tweet,

And life is a gift
To those that are neat.

So go on and ahead,
And don't trouble your head...

For in this meaningless,
Meandering mess
We may find the game
At our own behest.

The
Baby
Was
Born

In the house of the domestic Bun.

And
It
Sung
A
Song

In the realm of the Undone.

Worlds, infinities, and metaphysics
Are most
Appealing to the senses,
And the *sense* of the most
High and meaningful
Variety (with verité,
As it is actually
Pure creation)...
And that is where
Our host

Has made for us
The seat of great Vision.

Ah, yes, it is
A thing built
For precision!

A shrimp, yes, a prawn
Let himself,
To the dawn,
Become
A pawn

Which was used
For corruption.
Oh no, such corruption...

Yes,
The shrimp
Ate the bowels
Of the gimp

(So to speak)

As he registered
His lawn
With the treaty,
The wrath,
Of Khan.

487

Traps and routes
That we may or may not take,
Or fall into,
Or mistake
For the fated one, for grace,

Are there to tease us,
To taunt us,
And make
Our own little lives
Into tragic mistakes!

But still we can go on,
And when we must, laugh.

For without that laugh
(To see all beyond it)
We are truly fated
To a silly, empty hate.

I fucked up!
I did it bad!
I did it wrong,
Now I've been had...

I didn't know
I was so free.
I didn't know
What it meant to me.

A sallow howl reached for the gates
And the retard maggot felt the embrace
Of the yellow-bellied pansy
Who pulled up his pants:
With a frown and a fuguss
He made mincemeat out of rubbish.

Unholy!
Unbound!

These words make me frown.

I have become something ugly,
Something flowered
With a crown.

I do not know,
I do not know,
What it is that is happening.
I do not know,
I do not know,
What it is that I am doing.

These words
They come
And I let them go!

Oh, no!
I must stop!
I must show self-control...

I don't know,
I don't know,

Oh, but what if it's so...
That they must be said
For the beauty
Of the dead.

They must be so
For the tragedy
To be known.

I do not wish to hurt you,
Not with these words,
But they must be spoken,
Spoken because
They are absurd.

A trifling teapot.
A hungry beast.

I am the one
Who prefers cured meats.

492

I want you. I want you so badly.
I want you with me.
Oh, forever...

I want you with me.

Come.
Come with me!
Be with me!

Oh,
Forever!

493

A lion, a witch,
And one hell of a wardrobe.

I killed your uncle,
And your mother
Was a whore-drobe.

The flaying of the flesh
Of the quiet Compress

And a compression
Of the Capillaries
Can soon lead
To the next steps.

Once flayed,
Braise.

And then,
The pain.

For soon
She shall see

What was done
To me.

Incestuous creatures,
You live in your filth,
You writhe in your darkness,
You create your own bilge.

I call upon you now
To rise up with me,

To become and overcome

That most disastrous of deeds...

For now you are with me
And you are truly free.
I speak to you,
I hold you...

Please,
Come with me.

Not me
Not me
Not me

And that "I"...

Not that either
Either
Either

Oh
Or...

The shit stain
Forever remained
Upon the couch.

A sullen reminder
Of the weak
Little
Minor

That you
Once were...

497

Uncouple yourself
From this world of desire.
Become and become
That which you truly aspire

To be, aha,
And this thought?
Let it retire.

And then again
Go even higher...

To the beyond!
The highs!
The uplands!
The peaks!

Ahhh...
Such delicacies,
Such beauties,
Such treats.

Hm, what's that?
Pumpkin bread?
Alright.

Give it here.
Yes, thank you.
Now
I'll take a bite.

Oh, how delicious,
But I don't like the taste.

Anyway,
Let me tell you
About the human race.

MURDER! MURDER! MURDER!
Oh! Did you know?
State-sanctioned murder
Is, of course,
A rational thing.
And good, too.
That's why
I can kill you.

Death...Death...Death...

Oh, God.
Horrible, sweet
Death...

I hate it.
I hate it.

No, you've got me all wrong.

I never wanted anyone
To come to any harm...

I am so sad.
I am so empty.

All that I am...
All that I was...

Has fallen away.

No harm, no harm.

They have murdered me!
I have fallen so low...
I can't believe I didn't see

How horribly we treat one another.

The darkest desires in my heart.

Everything is crumbling
And falling apart.

No,
I don't want
This pain to continue.

Everything that harms
Is a crime,
Even art.

A whisper, a wonder, a trial of sorts,
Whereupon the fisherman
Became wet
In the shorts...

Did you know
What it meant
When your father pissed his pants?

Did you pick up
On the scent?

Did you make note of it
And raise his rent?

Yes.
Alas, alone, aloft, again.
The Pondering of pussy.
The Playing pretend.

I'm so lonely!
I'm so empty!

And everything repeats:

Where am I?
And where the sheets?

A triumph,
A conqueror,
A tradition for fun.

A mangler,
A manipulator,

A haver of none.

It steers,
It stows
Away,
Yes, away.

And comes
And goes,
In and out
Of the bay.

I stomp on bugs
And shrug.

I laugh
And cry

While countless people
Die.

Oh, haha.
Oh, lala.

Under
Becoming.

The breastmilk of something.
The tragedy of the mirror.
The misunderstanding of the clearer.

I am a pigheaded bastard brained bungler
And I live only to plunder

The prim pink pussies
Of putrid pea peddlers.

505

Everyone will harm someone
And something
In their lives.

Yes,
It is true
And terrible.
(These lies...)

A million infants
Have been burned at the stake

And all I do
Is write
And masturbate.

No! No!
Was it already over?

A mistake
Made again,

As if I
Weren't sober.

507

A secret something
Hidden deep, in this abyss...
Something real, supreme, seen through a dense mist...
If only you could find it! Reach it! Know it!
But to do so you must truly, truly,
Kneel before it...

490

The tragedy
Of a gazillion
Terroristic acts
Committed
By my people

Upon the backs
Of slaves
And "emperors"

And all kinds of packs
Of peoples and persons
And mild-mannered lads.

Untold terror
Lies within us all.

And just because

I see
And saw

A few foul messages
Or unhealthy orifices

Spouting some shit

I became
A worse shit.

I want to be
A good shit,
A wee
Little lad
Who cares.

Yes.
Yes, I told you before.

491

Ah.
Empty.
Free.
Returned –

To the primal state
Before I was born.

And the enlightenment
Of The Buddha
Is mine and mine alone.

I am a creature,
A kind of clone.

A lizard,
A freak,

With a thousand faces.

A monstrous child
With a mouth full of braces.

Untamed wishes
And naïve desires...
Make me an Untermensch,
A cowlick,
A tire.

Ugh Ough
Agh Eee!

Finally, finally,
(Again?)
I'm free.

I flew upon the planes
And undressed the remains,

And made myself a ghost
And poked a few new holes.

493

To relish this becoming,
This unbecoming,
This spree.

The body unmade,
Unborn,
Untree-ted,

Unlearn-ed,
Unbungled,
Un-bean.

I follow,
I wallow,
A track
Obscene.

A wild,
Wondrous
Brush.

A wig
Of wee.

Little,
Unfair,
Unmice,
Unmeen.

Everything must be done,
Even the stupidest
Of shit.
Even the most meaningless,
The dirt.

Everything must be made
To be as it is,
For this is the way
That it is.

513

Voila!
I stand!
Before you!
A being!
Not unlike a bean!
Not unlike a stream...
Of urine
And cream.

496

Oh, I must tell you
How it all came to be seen.
You see only through freedom
Of expression (even obscene)
Can we come to see
And realize
What he have been and might be
And with this
We need security,

And this place,
This home,
Has been for me
A great reprieve,
A gentle little scene
Where I can act out
All the most horrid and horrible
Desires and thoughts,

And say things
Without fear of failure,
And do things
Without worry of pain.
Be it for myself
Or for others.
A simple little vein
Of freedom of thought,
Whereupon I traverse
Even beyond my own lot.

Uhhhhhh,
Unnnnnn,
Begin,
Begun.

A lover,
A fighter,

A midnight stalker.

And hush,
Oh hush...

For what I am
Is what I was.

That is identity.
It is something like
A rug.

I fucked
And flopped
Upon four females...

And out
From this funk

I became a strong
She-male.

Ah!
Oh no!
I don't think I can say that!

Ahhh.... I'm sorry.
You know I didn't mean it.

Ummm,
What else?
Any other?
Any one?

I fingered my asshole.
I had a lot of fun.

498

No,
None,
None other
But me

Can be,
Can see
What I have been.

I and only
I, that's me,

Is here
And there,
And otherwise

Seen.

517

A saliva sewer sow-er.
Ya, that es waht I yam.

A peepee controller,
Ya, another maybe mahn...

Un-hung.
Un-birthed.

A belligerent
Be haver er...

Un Two ya Mater
I made muh
Muster.

The ends...The ends...
And the beginnings too...
Are out there waiting,
Waiting for you.

PHILOSOPHY

Everything.... Needs to be.... Very good.... Yes! Very good.... And.... Strong.... Really strong! Super cool and strong. That's what we need.... In a world like this.... And.... Maybe.... Something Big!

That which is (though not to exclude that which is not) *is* insofar as it *thinks* or *acts*. When that which is (being) ceases to perform such functions, it is then *not*. To be not is akin to the tragedy of formulating one's own deconstruction. Upon such a deconstruction that one which *was* (an important distinction to make!) is *then* (or ever-now) unstable.

 To lack stability is an ill. All before us, all below us, all you & I might see, is, now and forever, ill.

Sometimes I fantasize that my mother is a vampire, an otherworldly being of some kind, and I, her offspring, am blessed with strange gifts. And when I was a child...there was the thought that I could be a werewolf, living another life in the night that I wasn't aware of.... How romantic all that is! And this romance, romance overall, is really pure fantasy. Living in the world could be a fantasy, but with pain. In creating, we can make this fantasy live and breathe....

It can be tempting to hate people. It feels good to give into things like that.

The soul...! The spirit! The mind. The unconscious? The brain...? What a laugh.

So many things, so many words, and could they all mean the same thing? Are we so lost in our own language that we might never know what lies behind them? To imagine that we had no words, no communication...? Is it even possible?

All we have might be communication, in one form or another....

"I hate women," this statement is spoken. But what does any one man or woman know of *women*?

And when we speak these words, or words such as these, what women do we serve? What plight? What plague? What people? Is there not some risen spirit then within us that we wish would hold us, caress us, and tell us,

"Hush hush.... There there.... It's nothing."

And then perhaps it would, in fact, be nothing? But no! It is Something!

Let human feelings, emotions, and thoughts be tossed away into the garbage. Let animalism reign. Now everything is done purely and there is no judgment, only actions: actions for, against, with. Actions in themselves.

But let one man remain...to think, to know. Let him get inside our "brains" and let him show himself what he is and what he was. Let us throw away these emotions, then allow them to return. What would we see in that void? That kaleidoscope of sensation? Yes, more feeling, even greater than that which we know.

We can help others. We can believe that this is a meaningful, purposeful thing to do.

Do we do many things which we believe to be meaningless? Do we do many things which we believe to be purposeless? Why would we do them? Do we do it for ourselves?

You can volunteer to help the needy, the poor, the homeless, or you can help yourself. Should you first help yourself before attempting to help others? Can you really help anyone if you haven't helped yourself first? Imagine (hopefully you have to imagine) that you are homeless, addicted, etc. Perhaps helping someone else would give you something, some kick, some start of ambition, of drive, to help yourself, to pull yourself out of your shit-muck. But is it your fault that you waded into this shit-muck, or is it the "POWERS THAT BE" which pulled you in? Either way, you must take action. You must suffer against your own suffering (or perhaps oppression).

But this can be difficult. However, the difficulty makes it a bit more meaningful. Once you achieve it, it might feel even better. But there are people who are so beaten down, abused, shit-mucked, that they only hate themselves further when they do something correctly. This is the real shit.

531

The dum-dum world is ajar. They left the door open. All the ghosts are getting in. They are trying to do it. But they can't. Because this world is too dum-dum.

That which is, is. Being : Existence. Existence, the fundamental.... Implications due to the concept of existence: time, being, creation, destruction....

Existence taken as a possibility, not a certainty: "Why am I me?!" "Why is anything here?!" We can take such a moment to have awe at the existence of anything at all. Everything must exist as it exists for things to be as they are. There is no room for any difference from *how it is*.

I play games to pretend, to try for fun. There is no difference between games and life. The games we play are for the same purpose. But then, to treat a game as we treat life, that is, to take it seriously, and to take life seriously, is such an ugly mistake. It's grotesque.

Why? Why? Why is it that life trembles so as I place my fingers upon it, and twiddle it?

Yes, truth has been sought. And its value debated. But, of value, has this ever been stated? That value itself, and the judgments that come with it, might be themselves of a value negated?

To live without value or values. In such a life one would then need only to be. But how to be without value? A life of debauchery? But what then is debauchery? A life of grace? But what then is grace? Simply a life, like that of a plant or possibly an insect. Even better, a rock.

And what might pass over this life? What winds? What rivers? ....might smooth out this life, shape it into something so diverse, so impossible, so profound, so beautiful?

I wonder what we are capable of. I wonder what we are. But perhaps such things no longer matter. Perhaps we've had enough.

No. It's never enough. We must consider our own lives. We must make something of ourselves, if only to live.

But some don't seem to think so. Some seem only to care about us as a whole. They devote their lives, however meaningless it might be, to the continuation of life.... Oh? No, is that not the same thing? But our own lives can be forgotten. Maybe we should allow ourselves to be automatized, controlled, controlled by our own collective wills, and emptied, freed through a kind of slavery.

Amen.

The world could end. The world will end. The world will end soon enough.

And who will be there to *witness* it? Who deserves it? Who deserves to be there? What will the end of our world bring? And is it really our world? And what will happen after it all ends? Will the aliens live? Do they live? Do they think? Do they know?

What would a new God want from us? I mean us, you & I.

It might want us to create, and to create only for ourselves, since we'd never have any readers anyway!

If we throw away these distractions (porn, internet, etc.) we are then left with a dull sense of something...of depression, of boredom, of who we are and what scars us and moves us and makes us more than that which we were before.

518

There are times when we need to be sad, angry, vicious, even if we don't express it outright. (But it does need to be expressed somewhere, doesn't it?) We need it for motivation. To continue onwards.

Monotony is also a great killer, an evil. If things always continue on as they are, if we have constant peace.... We will fade away. We will kill ourselves more and more, in one way or another.

One's loins may determine much about them. One's loins cry out with their own voice. But one's heart might beat aflutter in the face of its own, in the face of the denial of the loin.

You and I might realize our *selves*, finally. We might become something beyond ourselves. We might tiptoe into that sacred space where "all and nothing" (as I am so fond of saying) comes to be, where all heavenly bodies can be found, where all that is and is not is possible, present, and continuing.

The path has been cleared, we need only to step upon it. There is an infinity within: it, you, the other, all. Soon enough a triumph will be had, but you & I know that a triumph is singular, and the process must repeat and multiply, extend.... For all that is must ever go on, and all that was must ever have been.

If I came down from this high, high horse.... Well, first of all, I would fall flat on my face. But after that...I would begin to see, look, hear, and feel all of you.... But not you really, because of course I'd still hate people being shit and all.... But I would feel the plight of violence, war, hate (in the abstract) and.... Well, that's it. There's nothing I can really do about it, is there? But I'd feel it, genuinely, and that is still worth something.

We are animals, all of us. Our thoughts are not significant. Each thought comes to us of its own volition, and we then trick ourselves into believing we thought it with a conscious intention.

Is it time to care only for things? Things without senses of self? But.... I suppose we can't know what has a sense of self.... But is it time to care for, let's say, plants, and plants alone?

Ah! It's so absurd, but so beautiful! To learn all we can about plant species, plant life.... To imagine what it might be like to be a plant....To allow ourselves the fantasy of becoming a plant....To take the *plant life* as a new ideal...! A kind of asceticism. A buoyant, vibrant asceticism of growth, stillness.... A simplicity of thought?

And what of the things we have created? And what of rocks? Imagine, to give life to rocks, to books (oh my!), to shirts.... Imagine our commodities overtaking us.... And not in some silly, critical way, as if I'm here to tell you all about the ills of capitalism (hehe), but to genuinely care for the objects around you! What if it isn't our lives that mattered, but the lives of the things that allow us to live? And all that we have made of them.... My God. That's so strange.

God must be recreated, but not as God. As something else, something new. A God, or several Gods. A "Godhead" to be communicated with, to speak with, to have a conversation with. With this, whatever it might be, however personal it might be, however deranged it might be.... With this, might we find a way again?

Cruelty can be so beautiful. We love it, we need it, we want it, want it constantly, over and over. It's addictive, cruelty, to be treated cruelly, to inflict it. It helps to be used, and to not have to think about a thing, to not have to care, not have to worry about anything except the next instance of degradation.... The flat plane of cruelty, endless, infinite....

The strangest moment of your life? How life lives itself? Lives again? Infinite moments of realizing things, knowing things, building something, your self, your soul.... And are you just a pile of shit? Are you meaningless? You forget your moments. You forget all your development. But why should I care what you do? Little shit that you are.... Alas.... So much escapes us.... Is it true what he said? That life must be lived for its own sake? For the sake of itself? Or is he just stupid? So many, so many are so stupid...stupider than one can even know...! Intelligence again is just another form of stupidity. Stupidity is a great thing. It is supreme.... It gives us so much strength to be stupid. The greatest of conquerors is the greatest of fools.

In playing at being smart, allowing ourselves the stupidity, we may become our creations! Our creations may fool others.... It is so good to fool people! It is so good to lie when it is in a game.

549

A child is meant to act like a child. A child is an innocent little evil thing. A child is aware of their behavior, that they are acting childish, that they are saying childish things. But it is aware of something else beyond this. A child *knows*. A child is extremely sensitive. Of course, a child needs to be protected. A child is aware of, senses, the intricate emotional, social, and metaphysical complexities of all that is around them, but cannot communicate any of it.

When does the child lose this?

550

Sometimes when something happens you can physically feel the sadness wash over you and creep into your bones, as if a rush of blood has pulsed through, signaling, speaking: "Sad!"

Yes! Horror and suffering, hate and malaise, but through it all an individual can shine.... A will, a will so strange and peculiar. A vibrancy of life...and suddenly the trauma, the endless oppression and hate, the never-ending "blanditude," seems it may have some point, some purpose.... And if not that, at least some meek little answer for the insane that still wish to live.

An answer for us!

The little rats, little couples forming by chance, holding hands and pawing at each other, violently leering, lascivious staring, at all the others and what they might bring.... We scurry! We crawl! Everyone their own creature.... This mass of mammalian impulse. We are disgusting. We roll in our own filth, our own fluids...and we are mindless. Mindless! We don't even know we're doing it. No, no.... We know it for a moment or two, we fight against the impulse...but we can only take so much.... We have only been this way for so long: thinking...creating.... And our thoughts, our creations...they are still steeped in that filthy shadow...they are still awash, deep in the ocean, given to each crash, each contrary flow...and we, we, we....

531

We have worked hard for ease and comfort in life, generation after generation has built this machine so that we might live without fear...yet now we are undeserving of it. We have lived long enough in comfort, us "chosen few," and now must return to "hardship," "toil," and "folly," for at this point it is all that will bring us *true* comfort. In this bath of meaningless, empty desire, a desire for more, for mere stimulation, continuous and monotonous in its search for an absent pleasure, we have withered away to halflings. We have become such "masters" that we are taken over, drained, by our own tools.

And now we must rebuke them, make them our enemies and shun them as if devils. The people might say this is merely an act of privilege, of superiority, (to choose toil? How insensitive can they be?!) and they would be right. (Haha!) But it doesn't change a thing. We must do what is best for us, we must give this life away (perhaps even give it away to the others?) and move again to our whole.

The things that we see can be big or small.

Time unfurls…. It reveals itself, it becomes, etc. The point is, time is a fundamental, a metaphysical point. All began with time, even if in the beginning it did not *move*.

Time, there, curled up into itself, accumulating, before it began its unfurling…. And then time moved.

Imagine several stages to time's unfurling….

First: Time's accumulation; The presence of some possibility becoming; A pressure forming from non-being (nothing exists and this stage is not possible as we conceive of it, this occurrence is outside of the "Earthly shadow").

Second: Time's first beginning; A spool of time begins to flow and *things* may come into being; *life* in the primordial sense, begins; *stages* are possible!

Third: Time continues and, unbeknownst to us, forms new beginnings at various points within itself, these points bring about new conceptions and possibilities of experience and may be seen when in a *world* which is inherently progressive in a technical sense.

God is real because I said so. And the big bastard in the sky says you're a bitch. Anyway, He is an all-powerful benevolent being who brings meaning and grace to our world and lives.

Everything is here. I see it and feel it. A thousand selves that I inhabit, all in this moment.

The world is created and re-created each moment by all that inhabit it. There are many beautiful worlds. Each metaphysical proposition is true as metaphysics is the creation of a world through its definition. The world is inherently undefined.... Well, maybe not "undefined," but unstructured, malleable....

We must be caring and thoughtful and true.... We must listen with empathy and understanding....

Oh? And who is that peeking his sly little head in from around the corner, with his short bit of a mustache and his finely parted hair...? Does he wish to be listened to as well? Does he wish for some of that empathy?

And still, we listen and speak...together! We silence not with screams, but with thoughts.... Is it so?

The possibilities proliferate, and hate and love.... These things come after us, chase after us, like dogs. We try to overcome it.... To drop the value yet again. But still our floundering passions, our pacified comforts, come to taunt us, and we hide in our shells as the shelling comes in waves of cries and screams for a hatred of a hatred, for a lie of a lie....

I *want* to be everything. I *want* to be nothing. I want to be loved & I want to be hated.

We want many things. And we get many others. If we believe that we are worthy of something (of something good, real, meaningful) are we then worthy? Our bodies do not betray us. Our beliefs shape them and move them. They allow our words to come out through our mouths and through our bodies, moved and heard in such a way that that which is within us (and look at the eyes, the squint, the smile) is expressed without. And we are heard.

Do you trust this? Do you see this? We can allow this sensitivity to come out – in some way – and trust our senses, see things in the faces of others, and then know, or at least know the possibility, of one being this way, or that....

Here is a little role for you....

Your name is Vloty Hachka.

You must speak clearly and strongly; you must believe in what you say. You are present and real; you are perfect.

You will speak the following words as you march in place: "I live and breathe! I devour! I kill! I save! I heal! Everything, everything, everything, everything.... Oh, what a bore! Haha! I love the world!"

Look at yourself and fade into me. See my face as your face and I will see mine as yours. We can become one. We can know something together. You've made it this far.... You're still with me, aren't you? Everything I am is in here. More than I even know.

You are seeing my soul, and what does it mean to you?

The big trap! The big big trap! There is a trap! That trap is…"I!"

"We must hate! We must hate!" What a dumb little fucker. To think that he knows better? Than the whole world!? How great! I bet he just loves to masturbate. And I will never hate. And I never have. I have only love and peace. I am all love and peace. I am still and knowing. I am God, and I am growing.

There are those high amongst the rest who are seen as respectable and intelligent people well accomplished in their fields, but are in fact complete and utter failures in that which they are supposedly so esteemed. We delude ourselves every day.

What would a new God say?

It might say, "the World is great and grey. Live again, another day. Try to take what you can. Try to make the impossible real. Try to do what you know you cannot."

Horrible days and horrible nights. Fighting against yourself. Hating your thoughts. Changing. Betrayed by those you put the most faith into, by those you chose. And then, you must start again. And you learn and grow, etc.

It goes on. You can live greatly. The real horrible things are senseless and have nothing to do with you. They have no precedent, no sign, no sense.

The infant speaks, "Goo-goo ga-ga." From this it must be affirmed that the child speaks nonsense, that it does not know what it says.

Yet, The Father responds to the infant in the affirmative, as if the infant child has spoken sense. We must condemn the actions of The Father, for he denies the truth of the infant's life. However, if the infant were to utter, "Yes...," whether incidentally or intentionally, we must accept the divinity of The Father. In such a father can be found a truth of the infant's life. The life of the infant becomes entwined with The Father's, as their subject-object relation (and vice versa) becomes so that the infant's being is completely dependent upon The Father's. The Mother is nowhere to be seen, as she is unimportant.

A denial may be found in the progression of life, the developmental pathways, as a creature comes to be insomuch as they travel through time. Yet, the past persists, and the infant and The Father continue even in the case of one's passing. We must not neglect the past, the future, or the possibilities of the present. For in existing as an infant, the infant knows and recovers all that is there, within the realm of infant-living, and The Father, inherently infantile, does as so because it is *expected*.

Naturally, we must conclude that The Mother, in suckling the babe, has developed an insecure sense of attachment, a *desire*, for the infant, and denies her own nature, disgustingly *becoming* infantile rather than *being* infantile!

The valueless life.... It allows for twists and turns.... It would be a thing which would accept much, very much. It would be good for you, quiet one, sitting there all alone....

Beneath language there is a pure kind of sensation. I'm glad that we are throwing language away here (after the book, of course). Once we're finished with it we will finally begin to see how it is.

I'll try to describe it for you, so you know what to look for:

It is still. The body moves. Each movement (not only your own) is felt precisely, individually. Scents pour into you, sounds echo and vibrate. All thought is only the repetition of the senses. Creatures, animals & insects, objects.... Everything acts on its own, yet together, as if interlinked. All creates a greater sensation. This amalgamation – this experience of all together – conjuring up some presence which is there, *present*, *real*, *seen*.

The Gods commune, and we are among them. They speak of trivial things we have all heard before. They look at us with glee, knowing we will speak again a great stupidity. We take a deep breath, and:

"Everything has come 'round to this moment. We cannot speak without speaking the truth. Every truth is a word and nothing more. We go beyond it all, for we hold values. We have principals. We will not give up."

And the Gods give us a good, hearty laugh.

In life, people must decide. It does not matter too much the feelings, the temptations.... People must decide. They must make themselves know. They must commit, because it is "good" to commit. Because it is "what one does."

We must make fate live and breathe, and give ourselves over to that fate we so desire.

551

Christian McDonough

Reality is a bit of a gag. It's not something we can really talk about or point to. I'm not sure it is an objective thing in the true sense. But already there are problems with these words.... Already, with this possibility, my ability to even state something with any intention fades away.... I loved the schizophrenics I met. They were such wonderful people. Their lives, their worlds, their reality was real to them, and it was real to me when I was with them.

Reality comes from belief. Reality.... The word is done with. Words are done with. Gone. They are stupid, have always been stupid, will always be stupid. *It* is, and *one* or *two...on and on.*

It's so amazing how much is held and known and taken from one's voice! A gruff, monotonous voice can indicate so much...and a high, nasally voice...and all the little intonations, shifts in timbre and rhythm.... There is so much that can be gleaned from it, beyond the intentional...an unconscious in the voice.... A spirit! A ghost!

575

Without value.... Is that what philosophy is today? Detached, reserved, a heartless observer.... What knowledge lies there, without any value? What knowledge lies there, without any *Life*?

If I were a monk, I would be the best monk. You could be one too, and we could be friends. If we were friends maybe we could tell each other secrets. Monks must have lots of secrets.

Philosophy

How are we to go on in the world? We need to make connections. To people and to things, ideas and corporations. We have to work. We need money in order to live. Don't we? I guess we all want to escape from working. But I don't think we can. We have to get meaningless jobs, or meaningful ones that still leave us half-dead from all that we then *have* to put into them.

The world is a fantasy. Does this fantasy please you? Have you seen the complexities in this dream?

Now, knowing this, everything fades away and returns fresh and new. It is so colorful, so bright and beautiful. All is so meaningful in its lack of inherent meaning, in its begging for interpretation....

We must abandon our humanity! We must abandon our "Self!" It is a scourge of vanity. It is a testament to our dead soul.

Perhaps I am becoming myself again. Perhaps there is that self within you from childhood.... The strange fantasies return.... Maybe it's only the limits you place upon yourself.... Perhaps they can be removed?

581

Isn't it amazing that we can experience a person, their face, as if it were a monster's? As if its bulging, bloodied, and yellowed eyes were on the verge of popping out? As if the folds in its skin were like excessive rubber collapsing in on itself? As if its smile were an invitation to a toothy kiss, a damning kiss, a fateful kiss....

(We have seen this face even in the mirror.)

The world, the body, the soul. All that is *is* insofar as it becomes, in the sense that it reaches its natural state and ideal. *(Why don't they see it?)* As living creatures of sense we may, for a time, reach our ideal state, yet we are destined to return to our descended state while our earthly bodies remain. *(Isn't it true? Isn't it real? All that I've seen.... All that I've experienced....)* In reaching our ideal we may experience the unity of all things, see the One that we are all a part of, and act out our destined roles as is necessary, becoming what we *are* and what we *must be. (I'm insane, aren't I? I'm crazy. It's all in my dumb head, why? Why? I need it! It must be! It will be! I will make it so...!)*

A man says that he is in touch with God, that he speaks to ghosts, that he has sacred knowledge, that he is being controlled by an otherworldly figure, that he hates his life, that he is scared, that he needs help. We disable him, we hide him away, we put him in a room with others just as scared as him to make him even more fearful. We give him drugs that dull his mind, that make him sleep all day, that prevent him from thinking, that don't really help. We don't explain anything to him, we simply tell him he is wrong, not to listen to it, not to think that way. And we then wait for him to die so that we might be done with him. Thank God, what a beautiful world. We do not have to worry about the evils of uncommon thought. We protect people by taking their lives away so that they cannot do the same to themselves.

All that is so, and so as it should be, must then be questioned as something else. For if such a questioning were to be denied one would then be found to be only a part of the world. *(A part of the world?)* No, no, a part of the world as it is, therefore unquestioned and unknown. For if the world were to remain as it is unquestioned, that is, taken without doubt, without elsewise thought, it would then simply be, and be within its own reason. *(But what is the matter?)* Oh, oh, yes, reason is good and true, but within such a reason there is no room for the reason of others. *(Then we must lie, fool ourselves?)* I suppose so, I suppose so, but there is much more to say....

What would a new God do?

It might do nothing, or everything, or everything and nothing. Or it could simply be, dimly, and fantasize with us.

It is all coming together. It is all finding its end. These many pathways begin to see their light and reach for what is coming. Yes, "Something." Something will be and forever become.

Art is a stupidity. Art is real dumb. But I love it. *We* love it, I assume. It does create things and push things, but I don't know why or for what. We sometimes act as though it is benevolent, but if we really think of it as something which "shapes our culture" then it is more akin to a kind of warfare. And it is a horrible, distressing, malignant, yet beautiful and moving, thing.

The world is made up of wills. Will your will stand anywhere before the greater will? Will it ever be seen?

A window into the mind will surely take some time out of your schedule. You see, some things simply aren't known. I am one to blame, for I have lived a life of shame. But at the same time another life was lived, and another place was given, to the little me inside of me, and the little one above, you see....

Oh, hoho, alas, it is true.... If I didn't know you, I wouldn't have had the glue....To stick to all this and say such things. I don't know anymore; I only wish for great big things....

To have the self-confidence, the trust in yourself, to create horrible things, make horrible statements, *play* at destructive beliefs.... Yes, I think for some it is necessary.... For some I think it allows the devil within them, which desires to inflict the pain that they have endured onto others, to be freed, emptied and neutered, into the world, without even hurting a fly....

I am a thing, that thing, a subject, an object, a piece, a cog. I am many things.

I live. I breathe. I think. I act. I do.... I have done.

I do not know what I am. I do not know what I will be. I do not know what I will become.

I am simple. I am dumb. I am above and below. I am here and there. I reach. I try. I learn. I fail.

I have desires. I try for things. I achieve things. I realize my thinking in this way or that. I see processes occurring within me. I try to change myself. I change for the sake of change. I try to show others my self. I try to show them I care. I try to create. I create. I manipulate. I recreate. I tear myself apart. I speak. I speak to myself. I speak to others. I speak to animals. I speak to plants. I speak to rocks. I speak to little things and big things. I hold things within me. I am a machine. I make and "make." I wish for you to see that I am here and I am doing this not just for me, but for you as well. I want you to come with me and know me and be with me. I want to speak to you and do something that has an impact on you, speak to you, personally, and care for you.

The great mystery of existence! The impassioned sense of wonder, of glee, in the face of all that exists and all that is.... Specifically *how* it is. Its own specificity, yes. This sense within us all, present deep within, though perhaps hidden.... This vague "Something" that we all might have, might obtain, or might have once known...!

The world is with beginning and end. Thus, we must have a cause and a purpose. However, the world is also without beginning and end.

That which has begun is without cause *(The First Beginning)*. To have a thing which has begun without cause is to have a thing which is infinite. For with no cause it must be itself eternal. Therefore, that beginning is infinite in time as cause of itself. However, yet again, there is no such thing. All has begun of itself and receded (eternally recurred) of its own sake, before its own sake *(The Eternal Unbecoming)*. Without having been as it is everything is without, that is, without itself, without its own sake, without *in itself* without.

Which then brings us to the end or ends. That is, end(s) as final cause, the end for whose sake everything else is. The end is singular and final and for it all is and is done, therefore, we must know and speak the end. To speak such an end ends with our own end, as in life we end to begin again and be renewed *(The Tragic End)*. In life we may then live with our ends in hand and go through it patiently to later be rewarded. Still, one must say that such an end is finite when taken in such an individual sense, and it must be, again, denied, for that is the truth. The end of all is then as it is, and its infinity must be recognized, yet denied, and all sense and reason must be lost within it, for it is not, yet so *(The End)*.

The artistry of the thing lies in its face. A horribly disfigured face, no doubt, yet still a face. When one approaches such a thing, bawling and whining, they can't help but feel they are being duped. It is not without reservation that the piece is looked upon. Yet, one does what is expected of them and sits themselves down and gazes upon it. How strange that it has a face, some might think, but it is essential, purely essential.

What would a new God be?

It might be only a symbol, but a knowing symbol. Something like awareness, since we are so enshrouded in "awareness" today.

Murder doesn't seem to mean much anymore. We are surrounded by little plays of power and violence and corruption and terror, but it is mere fun. It is a gag for all of us so that we might pretend to care, to laugh, to cry, to feel something....

Yes, that is how it is now, isn't it?

How would things be seen when there is no value? Perhaps they would be only a mirror, a connection, to plug ourselves into. And without us? Things as they are, occurring. And without it, there is that possibility that we could behave without limits.... Things would be *only* as they are, and therefore our creations could be things in themselves, not pictures which point, but beings which are.... And what else? The wire? The balancing act? Between truth and fiction? Between life...and fact?

There will always be horrible things done.
Always? I suppose I couldn't really say....

People will always do horrible things. *People* will always have evil within them.

The emptiness of all things. How *things* (whatever that might mean) can be drained, sucked dry, of meaning.... This in itself is quite amazing. That we even have the possibility of experiencing things as meaningless, empty, lacking.... We then may make a world meaningless. A meaningless world, seen this way by all, would then allow for all kinds of possibilities...horrible possibilities. But not so horrible when seen in the light of emptiness.

We could devour our souls...actually, we already are. We will allow ourselves, the human race, to be overtaken by our own creations, because we will it to be so.

What a silly, ridiculous fantasy! All of it is a fantasy! We have even written silly books, silly movies, begging for it! yet feigning disdain, pretending to be a "critique," a "satire..." There is no such thing as satire, not really. In every denial there is a desire. Haha.

But again! Again! I say things! We say things! And they can be dealt with, argued against, when taken as a world.... But who wants to live in a world such as that? A world of statements? Of arguments? There are much greater worlds awaiting....

A wanderer! A little dancing baby in the nude with a leaf covering his johnson! That could be you!! That could be me!! That could be us! All of us!!

People must be controlled. That is how we live. That is how we have lived. And people must be free. That is how this was made. That is how it all was made. There are contradictions everywhere, but not really. Contradictions themselves are contradictions (my god I can't stop laughing) because they can only exist when they are made to exist, when the "ideological" stance is taken that things must be logical, coherent, perhaps linear, or, when people believe things are as they see them....And even this, not enough....

Is there not a great logic which allows for these words to be spoken? A logic which allows for multiple points to coexist, intersect, and yet be completely distinct and separate? Disconnected? Yet connected?

Our lives must be pursued by others. The rat race. We need things to come after us, to try and kill us, in some sense, for then we will do things. That's how it all started.

We must restrict ourselves, hunt ourselves, but not kill ourselves (though I know we'd love to). We have made more than enough temptation for ourselves.... Good, now we give ourselves a chance to overcome it. Give us a leader to fight against. Give us a leader to hate.
Everything an opportunity to free ourselves, and everything another path to control.

The burden of flavor...of taste! Of care.... Oh! That great unbearable burden of living a wonderful life!

Objectivities can only be obtained through created human structures. Objectivities themselves are created via created systems (which are inherently subjective due to their creation by subjects) and found when empirical study of structures made within the confines of such a system is completed.

For example, one can make an objective statement such as "this word, 'kow,' is misspelled according to the established American English spelling conventions."

Outside of such structures objective statements cannot be made. Therefore, it is seen that the fundamental substrata of phenomena are inherently subjective. This does not imply that they cannot be known, it only suggests that such substrata must be systematically observed and compared to one another as obtained or learned from each subjectivity. Which is impossible, but then again, so is all science.

Everyone, every single person, is living their own life, thinking their own thoughts, making their own decisions. Just think of all they might be experiencing.... The possibilities are endless.

There are people communicating with a God. There are people on the verge of suicide. There are people experiencing the most sublime pleasure. There are people thinking nothing at all!

It is simply the case that there are those that are better than others. Some are born with a "call" to something greater. And those that are not as such are destined to toil in darkness.

It is the fault of the individual, not the world, that they fail life. Everything is of your own volition and cannot be attributed to outside causes.

The people simply don't understand it! They think they can have it all!

Perhaps here we can overcome all those temptations.... For power.... For pussy.... Here, in this book, we find an ambition greater than sin. We might go beyond that strangling world to the realm of "The Book," and there find the power (and pussy) within.

Things could be one way, or another. We can, in this day and age, take one extreme view and apply it to our world, to our experience, and it may fit perfectly! It can be justified totally! And yet, a complete opposite view may be taken and the same may be done with it. It isn't even very difficult. You could do it now. That is, if you know how....

"Life" means to be within the world as a thinking thing. "World" means that place within which we dwell, yet we dwell within many places. The word "World" impinges upon us a scientific way of thinking. Such thinking is antithetical to life, yet the words we use for life rely upon such meanings. Through our listening then, it is seen that three things are:

1. World is required for Life.
2. Language is an impediment to Life.
3. Language belies Nature.

Giving due course to this threefold fact, we may allow ourselves to see beneath the subterranean visage we are encouraged to believe in. All greater forces which suppose to overcome the natural world-life then can be thrown away. The truth is then seen as a wordless fantasy, and within it a blue sky, blue eyes, and white skin. The flesh is removed and the eyes are pierced slowly. The smoke rises and the sky opens up, a crack between its equator as pure darkness enshrouds all.

Finally, it is seen.

The fullness of a life when seen from a distance. The ease with which we can be so kind, caring, and thoughtful to someone when we don't know them, when we don't care about their lives, when we aren't *really* in their lives.

The labourer and the societal, all on the global scale, are meant to be existing continuously until they reach their natural end. Each society, even those failing or in decline, must appropriate their goods and capitol towards the end of continued living. An excessive amount of comfort and ease must be given up in the physical (and therefore psychical as well) sense. Our lives must be lived both for ourselves and for the world. (A mass burning of objects.)

Once we overcome and destroy the boundaries between all nations, we may then allow for the ants to travel to and fro, taking with them only the necessary elements of survival (remember that an ant can carry up to fifty times their body weight) and sharing it amongst the great hill.

I trapped myself within this life, within this possibility that I am now living. You have done the same, don't lie. We are on this path. We have made these choices. (Oh, no, not more bullshit.)

You must overcome! You must become! Something else! Something new! AHHHHHHHHHHHHHHHHHHH!

But it's true...!

World is Life itself whenever seen as the World *of* a Life. Upon this reflection, and the making of one World as above another, the Life is therefore lived via the experience of World as object to be obtained and created. Upon World creation, a true Life is in fact lived and may be observed. When one, from within that Life, observes Life, they create a distance within it.

Following such distance, multiple Worlds may be seen and further reflected upon. This division of World and Life is characteristic of Life's Nature, as it is inherently fragmented, yet whole.

When seen as whole and unified, World and Life may be taken as Existence. This Existence is itself a reflection of World and Life, as a mirror which may be used for the attainment of Life as it is wished to be ideally. That is, as one fantasizes Experience to be. The Experience of Existence itself is then the Mystery that is willed by World as ultimate thing.

There are many words.

One can take a list of words and create an entire system of meaning from them quite easily. We see things, absurdities, questions, confusions, and derive meaning from them as if their creator were divine.... Even if that creator is, in actuality, a schmuck.

There are things to do. You see? You have tasks to complete. Have you done them yet? Have you started them?
I'm working on it. I'm working on them now. Soon enough they'll be done.
What then?
I suppose then there'll be some more.
Well, that's good enough then, isn't it?
I suppose so.
It's good to know. It's good to have that.
It's all so simple now. It's simple again. I like it that way.

Could it be said that Bolesław the Wrymouth, and his violent behavior, was a kind of prophecy of that which was to come for young Poland? A warning from history? Or an inciting incident for the downfall and continuous succumbing that Poland was to endure? Is it not true that Poland first became divided, fractured, by his death? Could this not be taken as some kind of historical karma? But what kind of God would answer Wrymouth with such horror! It must have been some kind of destiny.... Some kind of curse upon Poland, the Messianic Nation.... While we foreigners are simply pale imitations of that one Spindleshanks, Władysław of Wielkopolska....

We can take ourselves apart.... Every time we feel something, think something, hold an opinion, we can look at it and negate it! "It only stands under such and such a perspective," "I forgot about this or that," we can do that with everything.... We're always forgetting! We're always forgotten.

So much that we might become! So much that we might be, come! Come with me! And you, with us! For off, together, we might dare to know, we might dare to show, to be and become, all that once was and all that we have dreamed of....

It blazes into our eyes....It takes us....It knows and learns.... A reflection, a mirror, of all that we are! Or is it all that we see? Is it pale? Empty? Bloodless? This face in the mirror....Their faces, their words.... A hidden visage of all that is desired in this society, in these pallid times...thrown into our faces and then...making us! Remaking us! As it wishes! As the machine desires.... NO! NO! PLEASE, GOD, NO!!

Love, love, love, love, love.
I am in love. I have love.

We need something to do. It feels so good to have someone tell you what to do clearly and simply. And it feels good to do it when you believe in it, when you feel, at least in the moment, that you can trust them.

Now, let's do this: stand up; sit down; flex your right pinky and frown.

You can create a place for yourself where you are everything. Where only you matter.

Can't you see how horrible that is?

You can build a self that is loved, admired, respected.

Do you realize what you'd need to do?

The way people are, how they act, what they want, changes constantly. But still, it's not hard to lie for them. It's not hard to be what they want, what they expect. But do you even see it? Do you know what they want? And the horror hidden even there, do you see that...?

The State may be subverted through idiosyncratic behaviors, creations, objects. Such subversion may lead to radical developments, but to what end do these developments lead? None in particular. Subversion of the State is simply for the sake of the deconstruction of the State *as it is*. For "the way things are" is always inferior to the way things "might be." There is always something missing in the present, and a future must constantly be reached for. We are not the only ones to recognize this, as the State operates under the same assumptions.

But then, what will occur once the State is untenably distended...? And can such an event really occur...?

A war is always inevitable, and only justified when justified by those who have justified it to themselves (and even then, it is only justified for such persons). It is easy enough to slip over into this *"justified"* state when the intentions are against "the way things are." We need this constant subversion and internal struggle (war) to continue as we wish, but also to *end* as we wish.

Forgive me, for there is still much more to come.... The laughs must not stop, the tragedy must continue.... A perfect place, a perfect position, will in the end be reached, for you must *come*....

CREATURE

Slowly, slowly, slowly eyes, slowly eyes peered back, and looked, and saw...out of a mass of nothing, out of a dark surface, wet and pulsing, bulbs of vision...and fingers, nails, the creation of keratin, cells multiplying, creating, recreating...a protrusion, a mass, blood vessels forming from slimes, oozes, green, red, brown, yellow...silence, overwhelming silence, a silence from which something must come....

A masquerade, a falling star, a broken planet, an empty bar. This was where it all began, and this was where it all would end.... Yes, my friend, let me tell you a sad story.... A story, like many others, about a Girl and a Man....

McDanus and Laik. Good and Evil. Devil and saint. The plate thrown at the wall behind them. The two of them on stage, bickering. The crowd jeering, crying, cheering, throwing plates. Their internal states: immense; beautiful; horrible. Ever-changing, rearranging, remade, redone. An infinite remake. An instant replay.

McDanus all sweet and like a babe, a wee li'l lad yet so big and strong. The Laik he all about weary and squalid and dry and thin, "nnng" he grunts. Each at their podiums, their pedestals, etc. Curtain open 3/4, red not blue. Cute woman in the crowd. Cute boy in the crowd. Man pissing in the crowd on the shoe of a child far in the back almost unnoticed but!

"My God my man! What are ye doin'! Put a stop to it! Now! Now! None o' that! No more!" cried McDanus, interrupting his and Laik's debate. The pisser stopped and raised his hands, cock flopping out and about and still dripping its last drops, by God....

McDanus jumped into the crowd, sprinted to the man (the man with his dolloper dangling) and fell to his knees before him.

"No more, good sirh ah! No more! Look a' yerself! Look a'all ya are! Please! Please! Know it! See it! Hear it! Feel it! And be gone with it all!"

The man zipped himself up and

Gongoflesh awakened to the great sun. He turned to his brother, Hongo, and embraced him.

"I love you more and more each day, Hongo," said Gongoflesh.

Hongo said the same.

They made love within the orchard.

I love you. I love you so much. I tell her and tell her, but she never listens. She never knows. She never cares. She never sees. She only lies? Yes, lies? All she does, all she ever does, all she ever dares to do? Lies? And Lies? And Lies? I shouldn't have expected anything else.... I know what I am.

It's beautiful here.
It's alright.
I love it so much.
It's a bit much for me.
Think of all that we can do here.
We could walk around, I guess.
The possibilities are endless....
I really don't see it.

A thousand daggers seemed to pierce the child's heart. The dog was dead, hit by a car. She cried all night, despite Henry's best efforts. When she eventually fell asleep – having worn herself out expending the excessive energy that it takes to mourn – Henry sat on the edge of the bed staring at the floor. He didn't move for several minutes, then finally sighed and went to his room.

A miracle must have occurred, for the open jaws of the panther were suddenly dulled and her lips seemed to melt away. By God, she had become the perfect disfigurement. And ecstasy was finally attained.

Fingers gripped the railing, their sharp nails ill-maintained. The veins pulsed heavy and blue. A machine whirred in the distance, and soon enough, the bell rang.

The children danced their teetering dance. In their lack of coordination something beautiful arose. No adult could lose control of their body so truthfully. They moved without awareness, yet they were clearly self-conscious.

A bat flew above. Chris ducked down, cursing, and spilled his drink. The others watched as the creature flitted away, then suddenly returned, and found its way in between the boards of the house. They were surprised.

To laugh, to laugh, to laugh. Why? Why do I laugh? When I am so corrupt, so frigid and frail.... When I stand here in the cold looking in on this tragedy of fat cats masquerading as people. These empty, pitiless souls. Except for, of course, my perfect woman, my honey pie, my sweetie bun.... But how she is corrupted endlessly by that rich bastard! Look at him bumping into that waiter so carelessly, making such a mess. I can't believe I laugh in a world with him.

Look at me, I'm shaking. I'll go around the back, yes, I can sneak in then. And I'll find her and she'll love me again. I just need to prove it to her, show her how much I am, show her how much I mean to her! She's so stupid sometimes, to think she could be with him? To let him take her? That fool! But such a lovely fool....

I should make a mockery of this whole thing, tear it apart with my beautiful words.... Such a miserable wretch am I, yet I can speak as though I were a king. And what woman wouldn't want that? Isn't that all they have anyway? Appearances? Opinions? Those little empty thoughts to occupy themselves with? What else?

Gongoflesh found a beehive which he entreated Hongo to observe. With a smile Hongo peered into the hive. A bee stung Hongo on his nose. Hongo collapsed and died.

Gongoflesh ran off into the night as the rain poured upon his back. Gongoflesh had tears in his eyes and wailed as he ran.

A woman, strong and beautiful and oh so elegant, she fucked and unfucked and killed and rebirthed that little shitheel like he was a hog on a stick. I tell you what, that bitch knew something. The way she moved! The way she cried! Goddamnit! The way she was! As simple as 'at! Look a'me 'ere, my buck teeth showin', I know I ain't pirty, but I do what I 'an.... Shucks.... Gee willikers.... Mister, I-I just wanna be loved! Don't you never get that kinds a way? Wan'in Louve...?

The tragedy will resume momentarily. Do not set your seats aright. It will continue. The deaths will come, do not worry. All suffering will go on as planned. There is no need for alarm. The trial is just beginning.

Young George crept through the hall on tip-toe, but still the floorboards squeaked. The light through the windows highlighted his blue and white striped pajamas and he felt exposed. His nervousness grew with each step, until, shaking and breaking out into a cold sweat, he came to their door. As slowly as he possibly could he turned the knob.... Then, when he was able, pushed it open. Centimeter by centimeter, inch by inch, with his face in the widening crack, his eye peeking through.... His worst nightmare was realized! Those inhuman sounds came from his parents as they embraced, holding each other in the nude. Life would never be the same.

Acephalous, the Dreary, roared about the empty dream of a town without a head, her small breasts bare, (the stumpnecker occasionally leaking spare blood) and was gleeful. She lived to live. She lived to speak. She lived to care. She was a good woman. She was looking for that man. She had something to tell him, though she didn't know what.

A massacre had just occurred, millions were killed by a lone gunman. He was fourteen years old and loved comic books and gore sites. He masturbated to horrific images on a daily basis. He hated the Jews and the Blacks.

Down the street, a father welcomed his child, Damien, into the world, and was filled with joy.

The world turned upside down, then back 'round. A few people did a funny dance, a man with a hat had them in a trance. The meals were given out one by one, the hobos sung as the meat was flung:

A washin' it down the daisy
A wishin' I were the world
A washin' it down the daisy
A willin' a whole new world

then there in the golden brown woods of the office. It was McDanus and Laik's, of course, and the papers strewn about held hand scrawled letters that could peel the skin off a leopard. Such beauty even in a single scrawl. The pens themselves works of art, their nibs flexible for McDanus who stretched his letters wide and thin, rigid for Laik who etched each ligament as if into stone. The images about the walls of fire, brimstone, heaven and hell, of light and darkness, of the galloping steed of pure white, its mane too, pure and brilliant; medieval horrors, depictions of torture with decrepit slaves in pillories as their asses branded; witches burned, their faces molten messes of smiles; limbs pulled from limbs from ropes tied to pulleys to archaic cranking machines; risen angels above the common, amongst the common, themselves the common; waves of color awash in abstractions that held all emotion, all feeling; etc.

The chair Laik leaned back in, his feet in black, weathered boots of leather, the creak of the chair of maple with a fine finish – itself a work of centuries, of developments once unthinkable – the thing pushed now onto its hind-legs by Laik, balanced by his bottom as he held his hands together and rocked himself looking at nothing.... The light from the window a brazen orange-orange thickly washed over his angular, sharp face as his eyes beamed with thought. The sun as if peering through the window daring to peek upon the man. The desk scuffed and dirtied and crumbed with fine particles of heavy dust, grains, meats; the legs of it ornamented with thickened floralities at their tops and thinned grooves reaching toward the bottom and finally resting upon taloned claws death-gripping perfect wooden spheres colored ivory.

The cute girl from the speech, Lithica, knocked and quickly entered through the door which groaned in anguish as it opened and she stood resilient before the unloving and unmoving Laik and after a good moment's pause he came out from his entrenched entrancement and turned his head to the girl unfeeling.

"Hello. How can I help you, deary?" Laik said with not a questionmark in his voice, but a period. And the girl cried out that he was pure evil and that she saw in him his megalomania and that his and McDanus' project meant nothing good, that it meant a civil destruction of society, that it bred hatred, that it bred violence, and Laik responded,

"Well thank you, honey..." and she then settled and comforted and leaned into the door, her hand resting on its knob and she

The pink fluffy cube half-simulated above the streetcrowds floated smoothly along with the parade. The molecular recreation above it, infinitesimally small yet completely visible. The clouds were dyed orange and the sky blackened slightly, for effect. The 'scrapers towered above all, filled with drones and gelatinous lives. Infants looked up, blocking their eyes from the sun, to see the coming pink elephant pig pussy face ride float, and float it did, colliding tenderly with the meat simulator as it spoke "eat meat eat," repeating this phrase endlessly. The actors on wires sung and danced, some, more courageous and creative than the others, twirled and flipped, risking a cross in the wires. The wire handlers eased the ropes into continuity so that all appearances were *seam*less. The computer operator maintained it with occasional bylines given in temporal increments, the many other acting parties continued on their own devices, the rows going on for miles.

The Witness was there to see it all. To have it be known and known always. With The Witness, none needed to fear. Though we would be forgotten, one would live on.

The Detective entered the building with his partner, Drellus. She commented on the size of the place, for some reason that made Mr. Detective chuckle. His eyes were wide as he took it all in and he hugged his trench coat to his body, excited. The ceiling must have been at least two hundred feet up. The whole building was white except for a thick band of cream on the far west wall. The rows of computers sat on pink tables. Each computer overly large and boxy, with wired components for jacking in.

"Ooooo!" said The Detective as he grabbed one, staring at the screen and fiddling with the components.

"Have you never used one?" asked the approaching woman, dressed in an overly tight, ugly brown suit with her hair spouting up like a fountain.

"No! I hate them!" said The Detective.

"Oh?" said the woman. The Detective stared at her blankly, his mouth slightly ajar, yet still smiling. "I'm Tralina, The Creator," she continued.

"That's very cool," said The Detective. "Could you tell me if you've ever trapped people in the computers, in some kind of simulacrum of reality, so that they couldn't speak out against you for some crime, say for some kind of extortion or something like that?"

"Uh. Well. Uh, no." said Tralina.

"Are you sure?" said The Detective.

"Um...Yes. You know, it is possible though...to do something like that," she said, trying to appease him in some way, to ease her own discomfort.

"So you know how to do it?" said The Detective.

"Yes..." she said.

"Could you show me?" said The Detective.

"How?"

"Could you do it to me?"

"Oh."

Drellus looked at him like he was insane.

As the struggle went on, the two men became confused. Why were they here? Why were they fighting? What was the point of it all?

Harry bit off a bit of Joseph's ear. Joseph cried out in pain and pushed Harry to the ground as he kneed him in the balls. They wanted to talk to each other, but they felt there wasn't an opportunity. After all, they were killing each other. All that they felt they could do was continue on; it wouldn't be right to start talking now.

Joseph beat Harry's head against the wet dirt. Harry grunted with each hit. The dirt was too soft to have any real impact. Harry wished that Joseph would turn him over and give it to him good and hard. Joseph wished he was with his wife Tilda and their daughter Harriet. Harry slapped Joseph in the face with a bit of dirt, temporarily blinding Joseph, and allowing Harry to mount Joseph. Harry suddenly had the thought to rape Joseph, something he had never seriously considered before, but decided against it. Harry beat Joseph's face into a bloody pulp. The windows reflected the light of the sun. Butterflies and moths hummed above the grass. A small village of spiders spun their webs across the small peaks of the grasslands. The tree gave shade.

A great light then rose before Gongoflesh and the beast, half-man and half-woman, spoke:

"I am Freesia, the Great Androgyne. I know of your brother's death and your sinful union. Do as I ask in repentance and you will find his life is returned to you. Head North from here and you will be led to that end which you so desire."

The homeless men marched in perfect unison, in perfect file, and were altogether quite happy. They smiled, they looked to each other, they looked to the sky, they were together. They were so happy, they made everyone else so happy. They weren't alone. Finally! They weren't alone! Their brigade developed quickly. Their plans developed of their own accord. Soon enough, they would take back what was rightfully theirs.

The Devil laughed. All was lost. The World split in two. Each hemisphere drifted away, hoping to find its own orbit. The Moon frowned, a single tear dripped from its eyes and floated into the greater expanse....

The Devil took out his cock and pissed into space. The Sun sneezed and coughed.

Kazul, the Magician, took his tall, blue, pointed hat off his head and reached so far into it he almost fell in, then took out a rubber duck and handed it to Blindeen.

"Here, child. Take this, and never be alone. His name is Fronchy, and he will forever be your friend."

Blindeen wiped the tears from her eyes and thanked Kazul profusely.

"Mr. Kazul, I'll never forget you! Without you my parents would have been goners for sure and my world would have never been the same! How could I ever repay you?" said Blindeen.

"Oh ho, don't you worry about that. Your company has meant much more than you could ever know, little Blindeen." said Kazul.

"Gee...!" said Blindeen.

"And don't forget, little one, we couldn't have done any of this without you..." said Kazul. And the band of heroes cheered in agreement.

"He's right!" said Horace the Lionheaded.

"You were essential! Absolutely essential!" said Callop the Calculator.

"Remember when you disabled the hall of swinging axes? None of us could have done that!" said Shalea the Scaled.

"Or when you fooled The Deathbringer into believing you were his daughter!" said Frederick the Forlorn.

"Quack. You better treat me right, lady." said Fronchy, "But if these fellas here ain't liars, I don't think I'd need to be worryin' too much, no sir. Quack."

Blindeen's eyes were again filled with tears, but this time, they were tears of joy.

"Oh, I love you guys! I love you all so much!!" cried Blindeen.

rose him up with her into the heavens. McDanus felt his perception begin to differ from his reality. Looking below his feet as they rose he saw that there was only blackness. This blackness seemed to go on for miles. Along with this sensation there was the recognition that the events that were occurring were beyond the scope of accepted, shared reality. He was severed from a root which all of humanity held onto. It was as if his brain had been thrown into the pan and seared. The angel in white, holding him. She was at home and her expression only furthered this fact.

As they came to settle the light grew from within them to illuminate a flat plane of existence which they then walked upon.

McDanus, hand in hand with the angel. He knew her name to be Juliotaintopas. His penis seemed to deflate and shrivel, to recede inside of himself, but he felt no fear. The thought that all people were indistinguishable, indivisible, and yet wholly unique was then true within him. He again saw the boundaries blown away. Creation was immense. When one created they stood on the precipice of those boundaries which were now nothing.

The perfect face of Juliotaintopas was still as they moved forward. God was a certainty. He could no longer have any doubt. Everything was lifted from him. The thoughts were no longer thought. All was as if unattainable yet attained without effort.

They came to a place of a yellow tint. All were before him and began stepping closer. They were coming. He felt a kind of tingling vibration within him. All sensation was thought and all thought was sensation. He looked about as they all came closer and closer. They reached to touch

The blackness ever consuming you, the viewer, as limbs rise and fall, masses form and fade away, dreary teardrops of gangrenous hate which fill the eye, oh, fill it! fill it! and let it be seen, the redness, the burning, all sensation.... Yes! Yes! All kinds of fires here in this pit. All kinds of raging, hoary things...a million, a billion, an infinity in the wind.

Patrick sitting quietly at the table, waiting for his lunch to be brought to him. Patrick was always waiting, always wondering.... He tried to think, but it seemed the words couldn't come to his mind. He only looked at things. He looked and saw them, and he couldn't put it into words, but he wondered what it was.... What was he seeing? What did he now know?

Wilbur the pig oinked and said,

"Gosh! I don't know if I'm ready...." He was soon to be employed as a breeder, as his father had done, and his father before him. "What if it hurts?" he squeaked. They stared at him silently and shook their heads in unison. He would soon learn what kind of life awaited him.

One entered the grocery store inconspicuously, then another, and another, each waiting the appropriate amount of time, waiting for the proper moment to strike. Soon enough, they owned the place. The fear in those Citizens eyes was palpable. It was their stench, their appearance, all that they represented, which frightened them. To Citizens, a homeless man was an anomaly, an aberration, a glitch in the system: a homeless man could never be trusted. And today, with a vicious glee, the homeless would prove them right.

633

My parents are dead. I can't believe it. Dead and buried. Look at them, their bodies made up like that. What a horrible outfit they put my mother in with those gaudy sequins. Who decided that? I can't face anyone. Stupid tears rolling down my face. My ugly, dumb blubbering mouth. I'm an idiot. What will I do now? What can I do? I guess I won't need a job. Me, the fucking idiot. Now I have their money. At least half. The rest to my sister. Look at her, she's so strong. Her solemn face. Her successful career. I don't even know what she does. And me, wallowing in my own filth. At least I had a job, for a minute or two. I tried. Now I won't have to try anymore. Why am I like this? Oh, God. I remember finding them there. I can't believe they died that way, in their own homes, some stupid shit with the gas lines. Dead, just sitting there. Their faces open, torn, perfectly fine, but stretched. As if God pulled their skin back and sealed it into place. The face. The face. The open mouth. The saliva dried. I'm so disgusting. I'm always thinking such disgusting things. Why? Why am I like this? What happened?

The neighborhood was sparse. The light was hollow, fading, bright, an artificial sun. My childhood friends came up to me and held me, they whispered things to me. I felt I knew them, truly, finally. I felt connected to something greater than myself. I was so happy to be a child. My parents were alive again. My mother baked a pie. My father smoked a pipe and read the newspaper, then smiled at me. I smiled. I genuinely smiled. I knew so much in only a moment. My smile came as if it had just begun, as if I had never once smiled before. I was happy, truly.

They must be stopped.
The Glorithians are already on their way.
The Glorithians too?!
Yes, I'm afraid they signed a treaty this morning, before the sun had risen.
Then this may be the final battle...
Commander...?
...for them!
O-ho! Lingor blesses you, Commander!

The tomb was dark and a bit damp. Everything looked like sand. The stones were heavy, the halls were long. The tiniest whisper would echo far along. Millipedes and scorpions crawled through the cracks and across the floor. All kinds of things must have lied deep within.

Somewhere, a sarcophagus filled with a mummified corpse of a king. How eerie! Perhaps somewhere, a light shined from within.... The torches were lit, and each step was heavy...those that entered were met with an uncanny, sinking feeling, as if they were being watched or perhaps in the presence of some almighty – no, not almighty – some draining, braining power...some disastrous kind of scent which gave no warning, but changed your life, bringing you somehow closer to some trifling *end*. The shadows creeped upon the bodies...the crumbles echoed...a million specks of dust in the air.... *A million possibilities, none spared....*

A child fell from his bike and scraped his knee. His father was there, trying to teach him, and knelt down beside the child, to comfort him. It was tender.

his person as he entered longways into the room that they shared, cordial and considerate he went through and with a slight bow said, as always,

"How do ya do, Laik?"

And Laik as was his custom allowed himself the luxury of languidity and spoke without response to the genuine inquiry of his dear friend and partner in their pursuit of that project beyond all passions,

"Back already? What's it like up there past them pearly gates? I've always wondered…" and he let his speech flow as if out the river and through and past the banks beyond any doubts, beyond any fires of the mind they spoke together.

"Ohh I don't wanna go on talkin' about those kinds a things no more. Not today," said McDanus.

"No good?"

But McDanus couldn't even bring himself to muster up another dance upon the salty-sweet subject and changed it as best he could,

"Anythin' interestin' 'ere?"

"Nothing new. A student hates us. Said that our work is hateful and evil and will bring about the downfall of our precious little state," and Laik felt it of no question that he should speak it smooth as silk, as he spoke all things. Laik had not a care about the ways it might rustle the soul of McDanus, who responded,

"My God, Laik! What did ya say?"

"I told her thank you kindly and sent her on her way."

And thus began yet another round of rowing between the two treacherous teachers of all, the two perfect pupils of a power, the creators of all conception conquered and conquerable. McDanus deigned to raise his voice:

"We must be kind! Caring! Sweet! Gentle! Yer ways of goin' about like this with fuckall care for what the greater world is thinkin' and sayin' just won't work! We need to consider what they're sayin'. Sure it's shite! Sure they're not thinkin'! But ya can't jus' go off and give 'em the kick they're expectin' from ye! Ya gotta listen to 'em, if only for a moment, Laik. Jus' hear wha' they're sayin' and repeat it back to 'em like, jus' to make sure ya got it righ'…. Half the time ya say wha' they're sayin' and they don' even know they're sayin' it. Then there ya go! You go on and say what yer thinkin' all calm an' smooth an' clear and they'll love ya!"

"You still don't quite grasp my soul, McDanus. The point is in it. It's in not giving them that comfort, not just letting them go on and about with their wily ways. They need some hurt in 'em. They need that fire, that burnin'! To really see it all!"

"Yer gettin' too carried away again now."

"Am not."

"Ya are."

"But, McDanus, ain't this what it's all about?"

"True enough."

"I want them to see how

The Detective smoked his cigar, chewing it and smiling. He was always smiling and bright eyed. He was so delicate. He was so gentle. I loved him, but he didn't like me. He preferred women for some odd reason. He could be so cruel. At times he would beat me, but he knew I liked it. I always begged for it! And the look on his face when he did it.... Oh, how it must have hurt him to be so cruel....

With a heart both heavy and freed, Gongoflesh headed North.

He came across a jumping midget, a man named Enoch who spoke of Gongoflesh's strength and bravery and then devoted himself to Gongoflesh.

Enoch explained: "For I have no life of my own worth living, and with you I might learn, for you are great." And Enoch jumped.

The International Homeless Military Alliance (IHMA) had effectively taken over the world. Their only opposition was the coalition of World Entertainment News Reporters (WENR) who violently argued against the IHMA's ban of all "worldly media," which was enacted based on IHMA's belief that such material promoted a lifestyle which encouraged the development of privatized residential structures (the IHMA was correct in this belief, as the WENR coalition was secretly funded (and therefore controlled) by the Legal Union for Freedom of Residency (LUFR), a team of banished lawyers hoping to set up a shadow government controlling all IHMA territory). This led to the great IHMA-WENR war, later renamed the IHMA-WENR-LUFR war.

642

103
Felt
160

There is much to do.
We better get on with it then.
What else is there...?
Don't start.
I can't not.
Everything is always the same.
No.
Let's get to work.
Ok.
Fine.
I don't want to.

This place is strange. The chairs fall under you when you sit in them. The filing cabinet opens too far, and I am placed within it. Time passes quickly then slowly. And I wonder how many years have passed in this minute. Walking through the office space...the walls are creamy. They're yellow, aren't they? And the way that face moves, it frightens me. How could it be *that* way, then *this* way? How could it change? The steps are maddening. I feel as though I'm about to fall constantly. And everything is spinning. A feeling is growing within, as though it will eventually burst and something horrible will come out. But will it?

"Oh, wow," said The Detective, "I feel like my life is over, but also like it's just beginning. Beginning again. I feel like everything has changed. I'll never be the same," and he smiled. "I think that should be enough evidence for now," he said to Drella. "I found a lot in there."

Drella was almost in tears holding Tralina in a chokehold before the shattered computer.

"Oh, thank fucking God," she said, and let Tralina fall unconscious.

"You ponder, for a moment, what you are and who you are and why you are. But you don't find any answers, do you? What can you point to within yourself that is of any value, truly? Is there anything worthwhile? Is there anything which has meaning? What does life mean to you? What have you taken from it? Anything? What would happen if you were gone? Would anyone care? You fight for something? What? Something which will fade away soon enough? Fade away within you even before it fades away in the world...? What world do you live in? Is it a lonely one? Do you think it isn't lonely because there are people who think the same things as you? Who have the same opinions as you? Who get angry like you? What a wonder that there are so many like you.... What a funny coincidence."

Christian McDonough

Your body will be unmade. A piece of you will be taken. It will be used.
What? What do you mean?
We will pull you apart. Limb from limb. Joint from joint. Organ from organ.
Oh. I see.... And then you'll use me?
No. Just a piece of you.
What a waste.

The Great Androgyne, her body divine, spoke to them with her flat chests bare and told them all that was needed, all that they wanted to know deep within their hearts. Her eight arms rose and fell in tempered unison, a whirlwind of emotion on her face as the slightest tilt of her head lent her a whole new kind of grace. Every moment was a beauty to behold, like gazing into the sun.... They were sure to go blind. Her legs slender and prickled, she could squash them with a single step. Her teeth perfect but for her left canine, so jagged she could slit one's jugular with it in an instant. Her only article a golden crown, two woolen scrolls bathed in blood hung down from it, teasing the sight of her nipples, on them her own ancient, fabled words: "UNFUCK. UNCUM. UNBIRTH."

I am Laik, Laik, oh me made a lake and a "lass" gone out with her ass gone out in the back and gon' and give it to 'er in the shitter and takin' it all gone and away and awash in the dust, the storm, the treachery of these travails as I'm all about and out in the sky burnin' before the light of the fires ah hell that made me what I am today. And goddamn they're gonna get it an' get it good. Them with their talking and speaking and screamin' around like they ain't got nothin' better to do than to fuck up the damn world with their wills of wuss and puss and piss, makin' the fire a grow and grow that they are and they not seein' a damn thing. I'll give it to ya straight ya sorry sonofabitch. Yer nothin'. Yer shit. The world don't care about you. And you you think you're carin' about it yes you do but you don't even got eyes to see the fuckup you are. The hate you got deep inside for your soul. It ain't goin' away. It ain't gone. And me all on about as a Laik I falled and failed again and again and I was fragile and frail and fucked in the head an' they beat me and fucked me and I did it to myself just like yous all and now and again I do I do I do feel sorry for ya and the scum pond gets greened and the willows do go a weepin' and I saunter about in the garden like a wet willy but I see that man and I know I know I know I can go on and be as I am and hate and have it here in my heart before him for he knows and knows too and lives and shines bright with love in his heart and it burns as great as my hate and I know it I know it together that we will show it show 'em and help 'em beyond me and beyond the shit and the fuck and the hate all together and by God the world will change we'll

He remembered that fateful day and his whole body shook. He pulled his collar in close and sunk his hands deep into his jacket pockets. It was a cold life for a man like that. No one could understand...no one had seen the kinds of things George had seen....

I'm trapped here. No one else will love me if I leave. I'm so ugly. I don't have anything. I will try. I always try. At least I try. I'll try and I'll do better. I'll be better. But I always say that, don't I? But this time it will be for me, really for me. It's not for him, not for anyone else, just for me. I'll get up and I'll get out of bed and I'll tell him how I'm feeling. I'll make friends too. I'll do something. I'll start gardening, and I won't let them die this time. And I'll take the dogs on walks. It's so overwhelming. But I'll try. I can't do too much. Not yet. One step at a time. First, I'll get up.

The masquerade so beautiful, all kinds of heavenly creatures, mouths open and laughing, their uvulas bouncing as they dance, the chandeliers piercing above, the flames flickering, the shadows convulsing, all such beauty here, on this beauteous night! Oh! How my beloved, my betrothed, is glimmering so brightly, so beautifully.... All that I could say! But there is none more to say...not about her, not yet...! And that bickering between the fat men in their big suits, friends of my father, smoking their cigars, discussing their finances, a big merger coming up, it seems, and their friend from far away, all dressed in red...all that they could provide each other if only their cargo count were to be adjusted, only slightly...Oh, yes, that's just how it goes...and then the disappearance of a few lackeys was something that could be forgiven, forgiven, forgiveness! Oh, how I wish I could be forgiven for my sins, most of them, anyway. Too many to count, some too much to recall, though I know they're hidden back there somewhere.... But firstly, forgiveness for my infidelity.... My perfect little princess! Forgive me! It's just that that demoniacal little temptress did tempt me so...and it was dark...and I was horny.... What else could I have done?! Everything so festive, so beautiful, why should I not have had another beautiful dance with another beautiful lady? Oops! So sorry! Here let me get that.... Ahah! Hahah! Hahahahahah!

Sitting across the campfire, Gongoflesh and Enoch proceeded to produce a great symphony of whistles. And such a symphony sang to the Heavens and called down the Spirit of Envy. The skeletal seductress danced to their tune and teased them with her shapely bones. When Gongoflesh then lamented the death of his brother with tears and a smile, the Spirit revealed her namesake, for she spoke:

"Such beauty that I have never known, I will do anything to have it. I will tell you that secret I was meant to hold even beyond the grave, Gongoflesh! The secret that will grant you your brother's life again, but only if I might possess your own and your brother's bodies in those most intimate moments and experience them as you both have."

"Yes, of course! Anything to have him returned to me!" spoke Gongoflesh.

And the Spirit spoke of a cave far off in the distance where a young maiden lies, a young maiden whose blood is said to grant the dead life again, and told Gongoflesh and Enoch of the beast, The Great Androgyne, that guarded it....

Enoch again jumped, with tears in his overgrown eyes, and thought to wail, for the emptiness in his life seemed it would never cease.

I found the letter hidden behind some old boxes in the basement. My grandfather had written it just before he died. It said, "Go fuck yourself. I'm leaving."

He was such a beautiful soul....

I stared at him. I couldn't believe what he was saying. He repeated himself:
"The grand wizard is my dad and my brother is their kligrapp. My initiation is next week and it would really mean a lot to me if you could come."

The sun blazes. The sky wanes. Piercing clouds, like daggers, fly through it. A mass of insects, mosquitoes, in the North. Frogs croaking. Grasshoppers stirring, yawning as the moon lives. Murderers hiding out.... The gravel is made up of hundreds of thousands of tiny rocks. Why should this not be impressive? Amazing, even? A burnt orange pebble, one hundred grooves on the side facing outwards when seen from the proper angle, another half-reflective so that it could blind one if only they saw it, again, from the *proper angle*. A home, more like a shack, dilapidated, the door cracking, wooden, the white paint chipping off, the indentations of rectangles intruding and protruding, making it as though it had a kind of face, a face that could look, a face that could speak...fires burning off, far off, in the distance...the heat pouring down like the heavy sweat that it brings yet a cool wind blows through and whistles through the trees....

Children pour through every once in a while.

I'm free now. I'm free and empty. Free and I have nothing. Nothing, again. It's so stupid. I don't even have any friends. It's my fault. The way I talk to people. I get too worked up sometimes. Every time, I find something to think about, fixate on it, and then I can't stop, I can't stop, I can't stop until I let it all out on them. That's what happened with Dick. I couldn't stop thinking about it. I couldn't help it. I had to know if he realized it, if he was even aware. It was all so obvious. I sat him down and told him. I said,

"Dick, are you like into me or something? I'm sorry, I know this is really weird. I'm not trying to make you uncomfortable. I'd understand if you are and it wouldn't be a big deal. I'm not interested in you. It's just, there was that one time when we smoked weed and we were in your bed watching a movie and I mentioned my feet were cold and tried to grab the blanket and then you put your feet against mine and said, 'here I'll help warm them up.' I didn't know what to do so I said 'Okay,' and you put your feet on mine and I was very uncomfortable and very high. And then again there was that time where you made a joke about taking a bath together. And then one time you asked me if I'd date you if you were a woman. And I was also wondering if you were trans? I think it would make sense if you were trans or gay and you were very conflicted about it because I know your dad was super abusive physically and verbally and I know you have a weird relationship with your mom and seem to kind of hate women. I mean, you said that a few times so I hope you understand why I'd think that. But, like, it makes sense. And I know you've felt really bad when women have rejected you in the past and you had all those really weird racist beliefs and you always seem like you're overcompensating for something and you always act hyper-aggressive and then if anyone challenges you after you try and scare them you get really sad and quiet and mopey...so, I mean, it's ok...."

She didn't understand me.
Who does?
I guess you're right. It's pointless.
No, I didn't mean it like that.
...I don't get it.
I mean, no one ever really understands anyone, not even themselves.
I know myself.
Well....
What?
I don't think you do.

continue on into the next room. There sat the commander of these subterranean operations. The U.S. government was certainly involved but did their best to make it clear they wouldn't tolerate any public speech from Laik and McDanus to that effect, so they were led in blind and sat in their chairs.

"Well shit. We makin' a deal for our lives here?" joked Laik.

"Laik!" whispered McDanus, trying to reel him in. It was clear to the both of them (though McDanus played coy) that certain high-level actors within their (adopted for McDanus) country found the work they'd done to be of a greater than marginal significance to society at large. And thus, (they had discussed this behind closed doors) it was only a matter of time until something like this occurred. They were prepared. The outcome will have already been decided by the commander's first statement.

"We need your help" said the commander, beside himself with disdain. And that was that. By Laik and McDanus' estimation it was obvious this was a false flag to cause an upset in Ukraine hopefully leading to a "continuous cultural revolution" that would down the state leader's culpability for the cessation of revolt against Russia's continued attack on European values. Ukraine being the cultural hub of European taste-making that it is, the supreme leader in terms of what is to come for the values of the "greater world," this little distraction would give just the set-up the U.S. needed to launch an all-out war against the world and give themselves a chance to get back on top again, not to mention lining the pockets of certain in-the-know investors with the resulting stock market plummet.

To put it simply: They didn't believe in the project. They didn't see its future. All they saw was another pawn.

Immediately Laik and McDanus agreed to the Commander's terms and got out of there as fast as they could. McDanus gave Laik the go ahead and Laik sent the encrypted message to their man in Poland. Poland, absolute war machine that it was so proud to be, would back them up when it was necessary, sealing their project into history to the great and foreseeable chagrin of the U.S. government, it was almost

A penis puncturing a vagina. A vagina which is wet and warm. A big hard cock pulsing with blood. A vagina swelling, puffed up, a pussy dripping with cum. Gallons of bodily fluids spooling out over the edge, drenching the bodies. Ghastly visage of bones creaking and moving, rocking, fucking. An elongated appendage with improbable flexibility, bending and swerving, lubricated to the max. A woman convulsing at unbelievable speeds, her eyes rolling back in her head. Black, blonde, and red hair in wet clumps, whipping about, falling and covering the ground. A man thrusting with intent to kill. Open mouths and tongues dripping with saliva, the noses spewing mucus, bile slowly released from the mouths, slipping between the teeth.

Muscles, veins, blood, piss, shit. A howling. Animals penetrating. Fur and scales. The chittering of a cicada as the breeding continues. The female Praying Mantis removing the head of her mate. Wings flapping, leathery, papery, unable to perform due to the moisture. Snails and slugs, worms, procreating along with the rest of them. A worm swallowed as an orgasm is reached. Endless orgasms, one after the other, pain in the genitals, soreness, unwieldy stiffness, tears flowing in joy and sadness, trauma recalled as the scene is witnessed, as the experience is experienced, receding into a dark, horrifying childhood.... A light burning from within, seen by all as ecstasy comes and goes. The waves of the ocean as life is born. The soup is electric, ecstatic, pleasure and pain as the bodies seem to dissolve. The cries of pleasure indistinguishable from the screams of pain. Anuses torn by hands, cocks and fingers, tongues punching, mouths choked, tits squeezed, everything sliding in and out and between and across and...beyond. Beyond!

Acephalous, the Headless Woman, wept quietly to herself, though she didn't know why. Aloud, she pondered,

"Why is it that I weep?! I'm not even sad! And how stupid and silly, for I have no sockets from which my tears might flow." She then laughed at herself and was surprised at her language. It seemed she could speak with a thousand different voices, all at once.

Altvehp was a weary little lass of a lad. A right little pumpkin bitch if you ask me. Always toiling about in the farmyard or sneaking about the barn. He never knew I was there, watching him, waiting for him to slip up so that I might take him and make him mine. I'd always wanted a little shite like that for a son.

Fluid, viscera, colors, an inkling, will, and from it, a bubbling, a dim glow, something real, something....

A tragedy befell Lauren. She was killed in a motorcycle accident. A short young man driving a BMW could barely see beyond his dash and rammed the bitch over. Her little motorbike didn't stand a chance. It was crushed, metal tubing flying about, the plastic of the seat cracked into a hundred pieces and Lauren's head mashed like a melon, then again flattened further upon the event of the man backing the BMW up to see what he'd hit, flattened perfectly, as if a pancake or, better yet, a crepe.

The great white peaks all smooth, the snow falling in every direction. There, high upon the hills, a perfectly modern mansion with dated interiors; a leaky sink, a rotten shower.

Still, all was beautiful. Everyone walked and heard their feet crunch in the snow. One could sit inside near the fireplace and be perfectly comfortable, but all would wish to be out there, to see that beautiful blue sky perfectly framed by the winsome Earth that they stood upon.

The silence beckoned, and was heard, and was welcomed.

A trial was underway. The Judge looked down upon The Detective, but knew he was necessary. The little gimp boy was in the stands cheering him on.

"Your honor, this man is a mess. Just look at him." said the Plaintiff, "He surely can't be trusted as a witness for Mr. Macky." The Judge, seeing the sorry state of The Detective, wanted to agree, but couldn't. He knew The Detective was, oddly enough, trustworthy. The Judge allowed him to speak. He came to the stand smiling, meek and gentle. He rubbed the side of his head, nudging his curly hair further out of place, his tie half undone, his shirt misbuttoned, snot trinkling down his nose....

"Thank you so much, your Honor!" said The Detective.

The throat slit, the bee stung, the body crushed, the lungs collapsed. Life taken, drained, away. The drowning sea, the lightning struck, the heart burst. The eyes gone blank. The limbs made limp. The mind racing, racing, and gone. Life before one's eyes, all events, all past, all future, made to meat. The great sights then seen. All beams of light. Colors fade and rise up to be great. Sounds, like music, like angels, like demons. Voices, words, hushed whispers and thoughts. Everything heard, and regained, all sought. The trials made finished. The day wrapped up. The night come to swallow. The tears made to wallow.

They then came upon the mouth of the cave, and entered.

The darkness began to enshroud them, light only touched their backs.

They continued, and could only see the dim light of the cave's mouth when they turned to look back.

They continued, and were in complete darkness.

They continued, and a dim light was seen up ahead.

They continued, and came upon the entrance to the resting place of Freesia, The Great Androgyne.

dark dark in the syrup of the night of the cave.... All spook and glimmer! Touch and dash! They slipped and slid slid about upon wet stone. The light from the cave's entrance dimmying.

"What?" asked Laik.

"What?" asked McDanus

And sliding down further in and through the cave. A twig on a wet rock on a stalagmite.

"Heheh," said McDanus.

"Come on!" said Laik.

And their majestic journey had journeyed them to this place with these intentions: to obtain it. And slipping and sliding on further down and a batty or two swooping about from above. They were very deep now.

"Ay! Laik! Look!"

McDanus had come about the entrance now to the deeper cave and, of course, it needed them to speak their spastic speakings, their words, together:

"It is all coming together now, to its end."

And it opened before them. And they entered...!

There, the munchkin Tolloper stood and spoke, his voice a mangled mess,

"Ah! I see...and now I must speak my riddle to thee...." McDanus and Laik braced themselves, huddled together with focus. "What is it that is red and green and demands a tree?"

Together they spoke,

"Christmas, of course."

"And who are they that move that mass?"

"The Christians, clearly."

"And what are you?" said the munchkin, looking at McDanus.

"Me...?" said McDanus, confounded.

"A dirty mick," said Laik, unflustered.

"My God, Laik!" said McDanus.

"That is correct," spoke Tolloper, "and when you have finished it all?"

"We will be done," they spoke together.

"And I...I.... Uhhhhh

A bramble about the land. The birds chirping, flying, diving. The butterflies, the bees, the mosquitoes about the flowers, about the grass, about the land, about the flesh. Laughing and smiling, speaking to each other, the people know and hear and the words come simply. Gentle moments to be forgotten. Simple steps make for walking. Telling one that they're a friend, looking tenderly to them. Saying thank you and bless you when a sneeze rolls in. And passerby waving and spoken to and helped. A cat needing saving, a man with a bag. A killer, stalking, but confronted and made to realize that his life may need tending to. And more, and more, all things you didn't see! You didn't hear, you didn't know, but they're here, in between.

150
Passed through
154
While underneath
112
As though it were
"104"
But really
167
Revealed!

Darkness and death. Quiet cutting, slitting wrists. Looking dreary and deadly. Not speaking. Not knowing. Long moments in the dark lying in bed. Getting out and seeing that mess in the mirror. Discomfort as the memories arise yet again. No sleep, not possible, not for anyone like him. Unwashed, unbathed, unheld, and unloved. No food, no water, until it has to be done.

I found myself at the hospital and as I walked through the hall through a closing door slightly ajar only for a moment I saw the head of a child emerge from a woman's vagina as she screamed in pain and it was beautiful and strange.

110
As though only
109

Felt
108

Do you understand?
105

Sadly
118

For 133

So, at least, with how I am now I won't get to make many new friends. Especially now that my parents are dead. I'm fucked mentally. I'm constantly saying I should kill myself in my head. I guess it helps in some way, but I know it's not good. I can just live comfortably now. No one is ever free. What does it matter to be free? What does it do? I'll be free and then I'll just sit around and not do anything. There're too many distractions. Everything is designed to waste your time. I'll run away from everything and be on my own. I'll buy a shack far away from everyone and let my dreams take over. I have so many dreams, so many fantasies. I always wished I could fuck a mermaid. I remember fantasizing about it when I was a kid and didn't even know how to jerk off. I'd just rub myself against the mattress and imagine it was the mermaid's tail and there would be smooth rocks and the cool, blue water would reflect the light and there would be, like, a rainbow. I'll go away, free, and meet the mermaids. I'll live in a world of my own where giant flying snakes roam and hiss and bite at you and all kinds of otherworldly calls from creatures are heard and it's like everything is a great big song. Maybe soon they'll figure out AI and have full sensory VR experiences and I can live there with sentient, sexy AI mermaids as my body wastes away. Freedom is just another chance to enslave people or to be a slave. What a load of shit. I miss my parents.

The Treaty of The Hung has been written up. Now we must commence the ritual. Is everything ready?
Yes, sire, the whip has been oiled and the pet is primed.
And the candles?
The candles...?
Yes.
Well, we figured since it was last minute the aesthetic intricacies could be ignored.
What!? You haven't forgotten the blood-soaked rags, have you?
Ummm.......
What in the name of Ladine-O!? What kind of Glorithians are you!?!

The Great Androgyne sat before them, and spoke:

"Finally, the great death I have awaited has come. The greater fate will now be accomplished as was ordained and my daughter will have her purpose fulfilled. Thank you, Gongoflesh." And Freesia lent him her neck as she handed him the sacred dagger, and it was cut.

I can't wait to slobber on this dumb fuck's fat cock. Look at him. This piece of shit better get me in with the Chinese distributor. Either way he was worth it for a little action. He's brainless but his dick works like a charm. Once I'm in with the minister I could get access to his international distributors. I could probably travel all over, too. It would be good to get away from this place. I'd like to fall in love with a Chinese man, that would be funny. Oh, God, what if that crazy bastard shows up here? I'd like to kick him in the balls. I'll have the dumb fuck take care of him for me. I'll cry like a baby and say he tried to rape me. Soon I'll have it all. Oh, yes, please, I'd love to meet the Chinese man! Haha! Yes, let me introduce myself, I'm Clarissa Wort. Pleasure to meet you! I've heard so much about you! Honey, would you get me a drink? Yes! I've heard you're very successful! And so handsome too...!

huh," said Laik. I repeated myself, but to no avail. This was just one of the many times I tried to get through to him. I remembered when I was young and had first heard of Laik and McDanus. They had a TV special in which they spoke with children's puppets about the world.

One moment always stuck out in my mind. Jimmy Frowbone, the colorful puppet with the big eyebrows, had asked the two of them about making love. Jimmy was puppeteered to say this very reluctantly and cautiously. McDanus began to speak up, but Laik quieted him. It was an uncannily tender moment for Laik, who most always spoke in derision. He said,

"There's no need to be so coy, little Jimmy Frowbone. Everybody's got the same desire, and though you might fear it all in the dark o' the night, it's yours to control. It's yours to do with what you will...."

This man before me was he. And this man before me then looked at me, cocked his head to the side and said,

"You were at that debate, weren't you?"

I smiled, for he had finally recognized me. I continued

Please 139
188

Please!

I saw them take her into the alley and they yelled at her and beat her and used her and it was disgusting.

All were slaughtered. They never stood a chance. History would never remember them. Their deaths would be hushed, their battle forgotten. They were destined to become no more than a tall tale a homeless mother might whisper to her homeless children...a ghost haunting their collectively homeless consciousness....

What do you think?
I don't know. It's not like anything I've ever seen before.
It's strange, isn't it?
Yes, that's what I said.
It's something important.
I don't know about that.
It is.
Sure.
It'll change everything.
Why are you like this?
What? Don't make me feel bad.
I'm sorry, but you're always like this.
No I'm not.
Do you remember when you found that rock?
Yes.
You acted the same way.
But this is different.
You're right.
What do we do?
I don't know. What do you want to do?
Keep it.

The Witness opened its eyes, and time began. The infinite was born, eventually life lived. And The Witness was, and it spoke.

141
143

But still 142
Within

Ever so gently, caressing the nape of the subject as if with the tip of the pinky, Faruth deigned to speak,

"Is it so troublesome that you...haven't been able to...perform?"

Werther was shocked! His eyes went white as he threw back his head,

"Faruth! What nerve have you to even think of such a question!"

Faruth bowed his head in forgiveness,

"My dear brother, I only wished to understand."

Werther walked the halls of his castle in shame, falling against the stone brick in fits of deflated passion. He was no longer a man, no, no longer anything of value.... His great power had left him.

But then, by some mystical grace, a vision befell him. He saw through a bloody mist that perfect body, as if a mannequin, the wondrous feeling, to be before, to have known it.... The Great Androgyne. And once again, his cock stood hard.

It was sunset. There wasn't anything stirring. I took off my jacket and sat down on the desert floor.

Suddenly, a horse came over the hill. Through the rays of the sun beaming behind the beast it looked as though the creature came down from the heavens to deliver that final message.

"Hunter," it might have said, "rise from that spot and take the final plunge. Go headlong into that deep well and touch the hand of The Witness."

And, as the horse disappeared in a cloud of dust and the sun finally set...

He's so weak. He's so stupid. I can't believe he acts like that. He never understands. He never says what he's supposed to say. Why doesn't he do it? Why doesn't he know? Does he hate me? Does he think I'm boring? Is he really that stupid? I should leave him. I should be alone. I should be alone forever. I don't deserve to be with anyone. I deserve better than this. I'm so tired. I just want it to be over with. It should have ended a long time ago. A long, long time ago.

onwards.

"Yea, ye mighty ones. How goes it now in the gulliver when ye behold myself and Laik?" spoke the one McDanus.

McDanus and Laik, clad in armor, held the talisman before the United States Chinamen. Their opponents spoke through their chinese jibber-jabber as such:
"You no scare us! No more! You die now!"

Yet the piss could be seen through their pants. The Great Wall of Poles stood behind Laik and McDanus, mounted upon their great white steed with Laik in the rear, gripping onto McDanus tightly. Laik's head spun.

Beyond this battle the Great Spirit had begun to take hold. The visuals were all apparent. The Aesthetica careened through all perception.

The Chinese-American Army swarmed upon their steed to no avail. To only carnage. Soon enough, only the Poles remained. The land of Ukraine settled in blood. McDanus had risen up and, with a thousand arms and in a blaze of white, he spoke in such a way so that *all* could hear,

"Yea, ye unfaithful, look upon me works and shake."

And before he, *opposed* to he, Laik rose as if a ball of fire before McDanus, and spoke just the same,

"Look here, all and all, the burnin' is jus' beginnin' upon the blossomin' land."

The Philosophicus Vitae-Creatum pulsed through its wet veins. Their film rolled on. The boy, Isaac, was anointed a knight for his bravery. The Poles pissed upon their new, expanded homeland. Death held his scythe out to be taken of

The heavenly bodies rest in their ever-present, ever-moving homes. The great masses of gas, light, form, and structure. The ever-expanding blackness is the ultimate comfort. Emptiness found, almost pure, as the fires rage on as midnight lights. The craters of the many moons, their pallid, white skin, their cheeks unblemished...they beckon their reflections to pretty themselves as stars. So hollow, so empty, yet so full and so real. The gaseous rims and the rocky bands as the maroon strips burst, dry, arid, crumbling.... What lies at their core? Floating, weightless, pure movement in pure space...everything rotating, shifting, moving...nothing stopped, nothing still....

The Crazy Bastard stands upon the stair railing at its peak, arms outspread, and screams of his love for Clarissa.

Clarissa screams and whispers to the Fat-Cocked Dumb Fuck that this man has been harassing her for some time and she is very frightened of him.

Fat-Cocked Dumb Fuck immediately confronts The Crazy Bastard, ending with The Crazy Bastard accidentally falling from the peak of the stairs, cracking his head open upon the rim of the fountain.

Clarissa then falls into the arms of The Chinese Man, and he is happy to care for her.

Two men were yelling at each other in the street and I think they mentioned money and family and then one of the men took a step back and looked at the other and then he took out a gun and shot the man in the head and there were little chunks of him on the ground and there weren't many people around but we all ran away.

Words coming and going, out from my mind. I am Horatio: I like what I find. How the trail goes on, and the end comes near, and a million little things appear and disappear. The happening happens, and the riot is grown. I could fear it, but I'd rather be gone! Again and again! What will we learn? Nothing or something? Or anything else? What unknown? What possibility? What future awaits? In the reaching for the depths, we shall all participate. Quail! Come with me! And be by my side! This here is true beauty...I will kill it with a sigh! Ponder a moment upon what you hear, do you know who you are talking to? Do you like it? Or do you fear? There is something coming and I will speak it true. I will show you.... I will continue to do. What I must. What I will. What is here and what there. Again, lost, trapped and falling, failing and figuring out what is there.

The matter was settled tastefully. Beatrice and George would have the marriage annulled. Beatrice would then proceed to the mental hospital and George would live the rest of his life out in a monastery. Everyone was happy.

I should fucking kill her. I can't believe I'm here. I can't believe I'm still here. She just wants to kill herself constantly. What the fuck is wrong with her. What the fuck happened to her? Was she raped? Did daddy rape her when she was a little girl? I don't fucking care anymore. I want it to be over with. This is inexcusable. She can't treat me like this, even if she was abused like that. I don't care. I want to be treated well. I want to be cared for. I deserve it. I deserve to do something with my life. Why can't I leave? Why won't she let me leave? Why can't I go away? Every time I try she just drags me back in. She always finds a way, the dumb bitch. Let me go, let me go, let me go and then I can care about whatever happened to her, then I can try to be understanding. I tried for years to be understanding and look where it got me. Stuck in this stupid fucking disgusting mess. I don't need to understand, not anymore. I want to go away.

I made my way to the morgue and saw the corpse of a man under a sheet and I lifted the sheet and gazed into his eyes and they were empty.

Creature

A massive tumor infected the Earth. All life became a cancer. Even the women and children, a cancer. Death enshrouded all. A great hand came down and pulled us under. The Witness to it all looked on, unblinking. A final end, and a new beginning.

They continued past Freesia and found the maiden daughter, Lala, asleep upon a slab of rock with the body of Hongo before her.

Gongoflesh approached her with the blade in hand and she awoke in a fright.

Enoch then jumped, and Lala swooned, they were in love and Lala spoke:

"Please, I know why you are here. Grant me a life with my beloved, Enoch, and I will grant your brother his life again. You need only to sever my arm."

Her arm was severed.

Hongo's decrepit body rose. The brothers buzzed at one another, the Spirit of Envy blushed, the newfound lovers embraced, and the great orgy finally began.

the office in haste and hoisting up above it to a reaching for Laik and 'Danus! Laik and 'Danus! Their eyes bloodshot red and dwindlin'! Each corpse created unto its own its self that been remade and reborn and redone againe and againe so was the blood from all to cleanse and clear and make clean! Clean! But none clean none so none nonces and nannies together with them as babes made so sweet and fine and full and…Laik thought on what had occurred but could not figure it with what he knew to be the case. If their work was the farce they thought it to be, how was it that, through the recitation of the last few lines and with the intention to bring one to speak, a person matching the given description would simply seem to appear? Whole crowds were devised by them in this way, whole movements were made. But, all of a sudden, something burst within Laik and he recalled that he himself was once an angel who had fallen. He once was against all of existence, and had fought for a pure *negation*, an unbecoming, and it had led to a leaky leaking of the vision of what one was! What one could be! And how! All of it simply that he fit himself into one shape rather than another. And that was when the dancing girls came in and shimmied and shook their behinds so care-free! It was majestic! Beautiful! They danced only for him? No! For McDanus came along with them! And he too danced and danced and danced!

And in the silent moment there was a darkness. The sky empty and black, the quiet whisper of the wind. There was a tear in the fabric, his shirt had a hole.

"Oh, what's this…?" But neither would find an answer.

Out in the dark forest it was cold. They were cold. They smiled at one another. They continued. He stepped in the mud. It was thick. The imprint of his boot was heavy. He groaned and turned to face you. He laughed.

The flesh slowly comes, out from the liquids it rises and congeals to form the mass that will become the body. Liquids forming into solids, scabbing turning into vessels, vessels into veins as blood begins to pool and slip through, within. Soon enough the pumping will start as a heart is created. Each quadrant operating in perfect order, this machine of blood and bone a triumph of will, of thought, of words.

RESURRECTION

Acephalous found me – her headless body like a man's – there behind the fence. The sky seemed to glow through the heavy clouds. All was real.

"Christian! You have finally come to me," she said.

"What a horrible monster you are. What have you done to me?" I asked, but she didn't seem to have an answer. She just went on about how beautiful everything was. She must have done something. It was all too strange.

"Isn't that your mother heading this way?" she said.

And it was.

"Christian, I know you think you have an Oedipus complex, but what you really have is an Orpheus complex," said my mother.

"Well, that solves that," I said, and felt completely blank. Really, how odd all of it was. A waste of time. Then Acephalous started up again,

"Oh, Christian! You're so beautiful! If I had lips I would kiss you!"

I ignored her. I had begun to think about something. I realized how long I had waited for this moment, as if this were an event to be set in stone, writ upon a tablet. How stupid.

"It took me so long to get here..." I said. And strangely enough, Acephalous seemed to understand. In fact, she said,

"Yes, I know. I was following you the whole time."

Strange how a woman could seem to be so expressive without a head, though her nudity may have compensated for it. My mother started up again,

"I'm so proud of you, Christian. I could almost cry."

It was as though I was being born again. I suddenly became so emotional.

"Better get to cleaning, Mother!" I said this only to help her, to lighten the mood for her.

She laughed and agreed. She always set herself to cleaning when she felt she was about to cry.

"...It's almost as if I'm part of the family now!" said Acephalous. The little bitty...! But I had become too reflective to react,

"There was so much pain. I remember all those horrible years...." And it was true. My mother comforted me and Acephalous chimed in,

"All of that's behind you now!"

"Sure enough," I said, "But it doesn't just go away, I still have a lot to work through." And that I did, and still do, yet Acephalous went on,

"But the sky is still so beautiful...."

We all agreed. I began speaking about growing up there, this was my childhood home after all. Acephalous nodded along as best she could, intrigued to hear about me as a boy. My mother told her how she would cut holes in my socks, how my sister would always try to scare me (like I told you earlier, back when I was still a "Dead Soul"). Acephalous would have smiled if she could, and then said,

"That's right, you have a sister. I'd almost forgotten."

And I said, as if responding to her statement,

"It's so strange that I'd end up here now, again, with you, Acephalous."

She loved hearing me say her name. My mother said I'd become such a man, but I felt like a little baby who would, soon enough, be held in the arms of Acephalous.

Suddenly, I thought how odd it must be for this woman to be nude in front of my mother.

What a funny little piece of narrative we have here. Oh? Me? And what if it was? What if that which is supposed to be fictional – maybe even satirical... – is much more personal than we think? I have often thought that that which is intended as satire really expresses a person's desires, jealousies, or frustrations. "Frustrations" because they cannot do what is done in the satire, because they don't have the freedom to behave in such a manner.

I have often thought to myself while writing this book that it too is a work of satire, but what is it then that is being satirized...?

And what am I? Who am I? But a figment that I have developed here, before you. A little bundle of silly ideas and "trauma" that seek approval and attention. Really, quite a silly man hoping to entertain you, to make you laugh.

But what does that really have to do with me? The physical me, my body? Here all we find is a semblance of a soul, but it could never be my soul, for "I" does not live in the world of "us." "I" lives in the fantasy, in the figment that is shared between I and Me.

734

And when I write a woman, do I care for her? Do I wish her well? When I place her into an uncomfortable situation, when I have her raped or murdered, do I revel in it? Do I take some horrible pleasure from it? Or do I weep? Would you weep? Would you write something horrible so that you might weep at it? Or would you write for pleasure? And when we look at all the things we have done, how much pleasure can we find?

I must tell you, the days I have spent writing this book have been some of the happiest of my short life. I cannot lie.

Clarissa Wort came to me once, and propositioned me. I turned her down of course, but the thought of it stoked my fire. That devious woman...all that she can do, all that she will do.... I walked with her through the park. She told me about her plans, it seemed as though she was speaking honestly, truthfully, but who could say? She spoke ecstatically, saying she would see the world, gain power over all, and then throw it all away! She was like a saint. She was entranced by the same desires as us all, only moreso. By the desires of the common as well as the uncommon; she wished not only for money, power, and success, but also for freedom, intimacy, truth, and knowledge. She seemed to think of her life as a performance, and she herself was the audience. I was sure she would do something absolutely insane, maybe horrible, evil, but almost as if it were a gag.

I have said and done horrible things in my life. At least I think I have. I don't know really. At what point does a horrible thing become justified? At what point can it be excused? When forgiven? What circumstances make it so that it can be truly understood, even accepted? Does it have to do with age? Development? *Illness?* And if no one was there to see it, not me, nor the victim, then what does it mean?

We must love how divided we are! How much we hate each other! How distant we are from seeing eye to eye.... Because of this the world is several different places at once, all at once, and all within one roof, one land. This one land which cannot maintain itself, which is quickly crumbling, falling apart at the seams, into many! And many, many, much, much, is soon to be seen, seen, seen and coming in to being! Hurrah! Hurrah!

I feel a compulsion to tell you things, to expose myself to you like a pervert. For some reason some part of me thinks that it will do something, that it will help me, maybe help you. But why would it help me to expose myself to horrible criticism? To give people a chance to hurt me deeply?

I do want to be hurt. At least I have in the past. Being hurt can be addictive. It takes away many things, many troublesome things, and fills them with something stable, consistent, and horrifying. But, then again, when the horror comes every day and pretends to be love it's quite easy to delude yourself.

Are you a little robot? Do you want to be one? Do you like to be one? To go along with things; it can be nice. I don't do it much, but why shouldn't you? But if you did so, but didn't realize it, what would happen when you do? Would you be horrified at all you are? But we already are.... For these machines have pushed us, for they have the faces of people, and all they tell us they tell everyone else, no matter if it is a lie or not. All the same, and all occurring, but for what? So that we might be happy? So that we might be free to do nothing? Ah, to do nothing, to be nothing. And all value easy, concrete, known, because it is the same amongst the machines, and the machines, God bless them, pass their wisdom down to us! Hazzah!

I love my life. That's what I tell myself sometimes. There are so many moments that I forget about where I've screamed, cried, wished to kill myself, beat my head against a door or a table or punched myself in the face. Then I'm happy and I forget about it. I'm sure you do the same.

Don't you...?

But wait! What if you've just forgotten about it? You might even laugh right now, as if it's preposterous, but just wait, I'm sure, soon enough something will happen, and you'll think all kinds of horrible things....

Are you a little soldier? A little warrior? A little knight? Are you fighting the war with all the others? The war of ideas? Oh, how splendid! You love it! So much anger! For they do not know what they do! They do not know what they believe! How harmful it is to the common values.... How foolish it is! How thoughtless! If only they could see it.... Proper, true! But, don't you know...? I'm talking about you!

742

Why should I talk about my past? Why should I talk about the things that have happened to me? Recount my life in obsessive detail? What good would that do? What a load of shit. I'm sure it might be fun, interesting to read.... To share in someone's life; oh, how beautiful! But that's not where things get done. How I have been marked, how I now behave, what I think.... This is important, and the past can inform this, but it is not the past events themselves that matter, not even their details (because I'm sure I've made most of them up), but what I do with them...?

Do you get angry when someone does something that you wish you could do? Do you realize that that is the reason why you're upset? Do you come up with little lies about why you feel one way or another? Or do you say simply that there is no reason? Maybe that it is just "who you are," that it is in your body, your brain? Well – if so – you're wrong, plain and simple. There is always a reason, often even more than one. And if you deny it? Your life is as good as done.

I'm constantly looking for something else, aren't I? Constantly waiting for something to entertain me. I want to be moved, shaken, but it doesn't happen on its own. I must make it happen. I'm giving up everything. I'll be an ascetic, but only so that I can become supremely sybaritic, and finally take pleasure in a real life.

You are blessed, for you are with me. You are something, much more than nothing. And something more you shall receive – for in this book, a thousand reprieves.

I sit and do nothing. What am I? Nothing. I don't have anything. But I have everything. No, I mean, I have good things in my life....

Nothing, I sit there and nothing.... It feels good to be so fucking bored sometimes. I want it to come out of me, to all come pouring out, and strangely enough it has.

I'm here, living my life, and trying to make something of it, really trying, and it seems like it's working. I might become something for someone other than myself, because for me I am already so much.

You want to live forever. I know that it's true. Somewhere inside, I want it too. You don't ever want to die. You don't ever want to grow old. You'd love to be forever young, and to flit about, worrying about nothing. To put things off, for then you could always do them, some time, later....

I will speak to you all and tell you everything if you come to me. Everything that I can. I want to be a leader now, maybe. I never thought I would be. People started telling me that I was one. I like playing these little power games. There's something wicked in that.

You wish for things you could never have. You wish for them and are happy to never receive them, for truly you want only to wish. And you wish for things, two at once, that could never be there, not together, no, not possible.

For you are a thinking thing (supposedly), and therefore you are a contradiction, an impossible pattern, an impossible *one*. Everything and nothing, again and again. Please, come and give it, don't just pretend.

How much of what I am is due to my *attitude* towards my "trauma"? – that past relationship.

For a good couple of years it seemed like it was almost all of me, except for my writing and art, etc. But even that could be colored by it quite often.... How can I even conceive of it that way? We are always the sum of our parts, aren't we? We are dependent upon every interaction we have in our lives to develop our behaviors, thoughts, functions. But still, for about two years I was almost constantly thinking or talking about it. I didn't seem to have much else.

It will never end. Yes. It comes soon. Are you with me? And I with you? The trial, what was it? And the face, did it speak? Have you yet heard it? You will, you will see it, know it, soon...! Trust me! I made it so! You didn't even know!

McDanus and Laik! Haha! Those wonderful little bastards! They are filled to the brim with my.... What? I...I don't recall.... McDanus and Who? No. No I'm not sure who that was. No, that's.... What was I saying?

We have become ghosts. We have died here, though we didn't know it. We have known death and learned from it. It has all gone beyond us; and we beyond it. We have already attained all that we wish for, anything more is just for show. The game has already begun. The time has already passed. Always know this, know it now, and before, and before that which comes. You are ready. It is about to be seen. It already was, but now you know.

I will it all. I will myself to my own ends. I want to change myself continuously, over time, and become several different people throughout my life. I even believe you could be an infinite number of people at once, if only for a few brief moments. Who am I now? Not even "I" know. I see everything before me, yet I feel nothing! But that's stupid. I don't need it. I don't need anything.

I want my art to change. There's no need for a consistent style. That's just falling into the trap of self-commodification. (Or is it simply self-creation?) Think of all the new things that I can do. All that I could create. And when I do it all and look back upon my life, upon myself, what will I see? Will it be glorious, brilliant, and bright! – or simply a mess?

I can do it all. I can do anything. I'm a genius, don't you see? I am so beautiful, so wild, so free. What can you do? What have you done? Why do you limit yourself? You know, that isn't much fun....

I speak. I say "I." I can believe that I am creating a new lifeform, a living organism, through this book. I can believe it sincerely, and then it is real. It's real for me. It's real enough. I've known people who believed things like this. You would call them delusional or crazy, you would pity them, feel sad for them, but why should you? Yes, I do feel for them. I do worry about the stress, the anxiety, the pain they go through, but I do not listen to the things they say, the things they believe, and pout and say, "Oh, you poor thing...."

What do you want from me? Why are you here? Why are you still here? Why have you stayed with me this far? Do you like it? Do you like it here? Is this a nice place for you? Are you excited to reach the end with me? The end, the great end! To find something! To have something, together! Oh! We will be together, together forever! Once it is all over I will never leave you.... And perhaps you will never leave me?

758

I say "I," and I mean nothing by it, I'm sure. These stupid words I use.... Sometimes I'll get caught on a word and find myself using it again and again. Why? Sometimes I'll try to say something, something in my head, and it is there, and real, and clear, but it doesn't come out. I can't put it into words. Why? What was it that was there?

I am simply a thing that acts. This body, this mind, functions and operates, and to make it easier it says "I," and it tries to think for "itself," and it feels good about "itself" when it feels like "I."

I am writing to create myself. I am also living to create myself, also to destroy myself. I can attribute my thoughts and behaviors to any number of things at any time. The more I search for reasons, the more I find. I am a man because I was socially programmed to be this way. I am a woman because I deny that I am a woman. I want friends because I am insecure. I want to be smart so that I will be better than everyone. I want to be better than everyone because I think I'm worthless. I think I'm worthless because I didn't know how to talk to people when I was young. I didn't know how to talk to people because nobody taught me. Nobody taught me because they didn't know how. Nobody knew how because *they* were neglected. *I* was neglected because I was inherently anxious. I was inherently anxious because of my brain chemicals. I stopped being anxious because I didn't believe in my brain chemicals. All of this equally true, meaningless, and false. And each could give me a lifetime's worth of material to dissect and contemplate, and I would genuinely learn so much about myself through this contemplation and genuinely improve in my daily life, in my thinking, in my being. But in what way? And in what ways would I be hurt by it? For we are hurt and helped in equal measure by all things. We gain and lose at the same rate. But yet again, in what way? What hurts? What helps? Well, it must depend on who you are. And why are you who you are? Because of your parents. And why them? Because you are attached to them. And why are you attached to them? Because of your disorder. And why do you have a disorder? Because it isn't normal. And why isn't it normal? Because they don't talk about it. And why don't they talk about it? Because it...

I don't believe in mental illness. Ok, maybe I do. But not so much. It's mostly made up bullshit. Don't even start about the brain. There's no such thing as a neurodivergent. What the hell is a normal brain supposed to look like? Where is the divergence? Can you tell me where it is divergent? In what sense? What chemicals? What brain structure? And how many brains has this brain been compared to? And how did they observe this brain? Was it living? Did they cut it open? How limited was the machinery? How precise?

But anyway, people need help, not medication. Some people get help from medication. Most people are fucked by it. Everyone is dependent upon constant, endless streams of bullshit. Our computers are medication. Our medications cause need for further medication. But medication does help. I've been on it before, it helped me immensely. But ask questions. Look things up for yourself. Don't put blind faith in a psychiatrist, they don't even believe in human beings!

I don't know. Live your own life. I don't care. I care for me and the people I care about.

Why should I even care who I am? Why should I say things that I believe? I don't want to believe in anything. I don't want to think. It's just another way to be fooled, it's just another trap. Yes! This could be who I am! Nonsense! Nonself! I don't care! I don't give a shit!

Have you thought about your life? About what you want to do? What you want to be? Do you care for things? Do you have something you want to do? What is it? Please, tell me. What do you want? What do you do all day? Do you hold yourself back? I hate it when people want to do something but some sense of embarrassment holds them back. You can do whatever you like. Just look at the horrible, deranged things I've said here. Why don't you do it? Whatever it is....

Why shouldn't I believe in irrational things?

It is the only way to push further. It is the only way to achieve new things, things previously thought impossible.

But of course, we need to come back down to Earth and hate ourselves every once in a while, right?

A million different moments in but a single second. That is what we are capable of. That is something you have experienced, just like me. Everything is there. If only we had the speed to let it all out...to simply go and go with no real regard for what is said. It will take care of itself. It does much more than you realize. It functions, it forms.... At least, that's what it does for me.

Are you there now? Are you looking at yourself? Are you aware that you are here in this moment with me, with yourself, with your thoughts, with your body? What does it mean to you? It will mean nothing if you ask it like that. You must create meanings. I used to come up with all kinds of nonsense meaning and it felt horrible. It was awful. I was deluding myself constantly. But sometimes I will try and something genuine will seem to come. Some real sense of meaning. But what is the difference between this deranged sense and this meaningful sense? Is there really any difference? And if I wasn't trying, if I wasn't looking for it, could I ever have found it?

I am alive again. I am free. I hate how much I love myself.

I am free, but from what? Not from myself. I am always trapped within myself, except, perhaps, for a few moments which might come in my future where I might seem to see things as someone else, as something else, as though they were really there, and my mind might be gone and the colors might be bright.

Everything I am is with you.
Everything I am is in you.

Resurrection

The Detective smiled his golden smile at me. I couldn't help but smile in return. I wondered what horrors he might pull out of me with that smile, but I didn't fear it.

"You're a bit of a pervert, aren't you?" he said.

I gave it up freely,

"You got me, Detective! I'm disgusting! You can't imagine the sexual schemes, scenarios, roles, etc., that I'd come up with in the bedroom if given the chance!"

The Detective raised his eyebrows and pursed his lips. I think he was having fun; I was hoping he would. He asked me for details and I whispered a few into his ear. He blushed! I told him I'd much rather go on some kind of wild cyberpunk-esque noir mystery with him, maybe with alternate realities, or at least with highly complex virtual ones, and he went on at length about how much he hated high-concept bullshit that fucks with his head, but still he smiled.

I remember once I was very young and I had all kinds of silly ideas about the world. I thought it was round and beautiful and held life in it – how silly. I know now that everything is completely idiotic and stupid and a lie. And there are no facts. There are no thoughts. We are little animals that prey upon each other, vampires that suck the life force from one another through things like "social skills" and "reason."

I never want to die. I want to live forever. If I live forever I can keep writing, creating things, learning things, and become something more. And everyone else can too, and we won't be special but it won't matter, we'll all be old enough that we'll have had time to get over it.

But people never grow, people never get over things.

What do you mean to yourself? What will you think when you die? Will you be happy? Will you be sad? You will die. You are going to die. Hopefully. God willing. And will you have failed?

I'm a liar. But it's only a game. I create life, but it's only for fun. I have a name, I am Christian McDonough. That's my name! Christian Luke McDonough! That's my name and I wouldn't give it up for anything in the world. I'm done with loving myself, it's time to love everything else. Yes! I love the rape, murder, extortion, corruption, filth, disease, disasters of this world! God...!

I like to pretend that I know things. I also like to pretend that I know nothing. It can be so good to feel you know nothing. It's very freeing. If you know nothing you can really get away with a lot.

Who are my friends? I have all kinds of friends. So many friends, friends that would never hurt me, never betray me, never lie to me.
But I don't mind evil people. No, I don't mind.

I pray to The Great Androgyne every day. (Cum.)

We must free ourselves from ourselves. Be like me, become nonsensical and non-rational, at least for a day or even only a moment....

It's a maddening feeling, a horrible vicious energy. Once we free ourselves from ourselves – and from our distractions, our comforts – we can start to create and accept and reject. I love rejecting things, even people. Though I don't do it too often. It's so good to get rid of people.

What? What am I saying?

Have you ever even lived? Have you made the world? Have you questioned the world? Have you asked yourself those silly questions? Those simple things? Why is everything the way that it is? Why is there something rather than nothing? Why was I born as this person rather than another? Stupid questions like this, profound yet banal, are necessary. Have you begun the journey? The process? If you look, you will see yourself change over time. That is, if you're doing it. Make sure that you're doing it. Don't worry, I'm with you.

I love my girlfriend. She's so beautiful and pretty and opinionated and fun. She's so strong.

I speak my mind to all who will listen. The trouble is that no one wants to listen to me. Why do they ignore me? I'm so tired of people pretending that things are fine, of people lying because they don't want to make anyone uncomfortable, because they're scared of the social implications of the truth.

    (I meant this simply on an individual level! Like two people getting coffee and one doesn't want to admit to disliking the others shirt! Things like that!)

Christian McDonough

What am I doing to myself? Why am I doing this? What is happening?
What will happen?

I wish, sometimes, to be seen only as a victim. When a misunderstanding arises that makes me out to be much weaker than I am, makes it seem as though I have endured much more than I have, some part of me lights up and my face becomes a soft putty to be molded into the image of a little doe, an infant, who needs to be protected.

And soon enough, I am!

Perhaps because of my wish to be a victim, I also wish to be an assailant. To hurt others, to show them that I am not weak, that I do not need to be babied. And even this "playing the victim" can be seen as the act of an assailant! It is strategic, in some cases, and from it I can get what I want.

I was raped viciously when I was young by a man with a clown's face, a clown's nose. He looked deeply into my eyes and, for some reason, I couldn't look away. I cried and cried. I was nothing again. And still, I can be everything. He honked his horn when I went away, far away. And from there a new life seemed to begin. I had forgotten it all until this very moment. I write to you, oh, how I write to you....

There's no need for me to be here. I am not here. I don't exist. I have ceased to exist. I am speaking very genuinely now. I am not here. I'm frightened. I wish I were here, but I'm not. How can this be? How can I believe this? Oh, wait, I don't have to.

The processes of people that you can be, they're endless. We'll discuss them more later. Just think. You were a child. What kind of a child were you? Were you quiet? Were you loud? But inside, what was happening? What was there? And now? This growth can continue indefinitely. But is it really growth, or just change? But you don't want to change, do you?

I remember staring into a black hole, out in the vacuum of space, and saying to myself, "you know, it's odd looking at something like this. It's pure death. I thought it might be cooler, but it's just death. It just ends things, really." It's a good memory. That was when I finally realized what death was like, at least, the moment of death. I don't know what would happen afterwards. I think there would be some kind of experience, at least for a moment or two, just a little bit...or some kind of ridiculous Heaven where we all have wings and sings songs on clouds...that could be it too.

I am a liar! God bless me, for I am a liar! And among liars, a saint. A free spirit here, dancing with my fingers crossed. I have no need for truth, nor value, nor thought...nor even life. I dance here, I write to you, for I am awaiting death. No! Not even that! I am inviting death with each word I write: I am entertaining death. I am making it come nearer, closer and closer with each word. And I am with it, understanding it, building it. I am building a death for myself. Perhaps I'll kill myself before you all. My final act! These words, all that I create, will be with me and inform my death: fill it and make it full. They will engender the experience of death, and all that I have written will be experienced as life, in death!

I have killed myself over a hundred times. I know what real suffering is. It feels good to be able to hold that over people, if I wanted to. It feels good to know that I don't want to.

Dying was very horrifying, then peaceful. I think you get the idea. If you pay more attention to your emotions, your feelings, you can get a good sense of what extreme experiences might be like. You'd need to talk about them, write about them, generally just devote a lot of attention to them...be a bit self-obsessed, at least for a little while.

Do I want only to impress you? Am I so weak and stupid as to want something like that? Do you care what others think of you? Do you think it matters? My body, my blue eyes, my ten fingers, my ten toes. I used to be a little shrimp, so skinny, lanky, but now I am so big, brawny...but not so big, no, not so big.... But still, it feels as if I'm unwieldy. I look at myself in the mirror and I am surprised at what I see. Was I always like this? Was I always so round? My face, it's like a child's. But with a beard I look strong. But underneath...such a sensitive, soft little pudge. What of your face? What do you make of it? Is it any good? I'm sure you hate it, especially if you're a woman. Your body? Do you hate your body? Do you want to change just one or two little things about it? No, no, give it up. It'll never be any good. Just accept it. Just love it. Just love who you are. Just love the way you look. Don't even look at yourself, you don't need to. Just take care of yourself. And be.

It is only in my hatred that my love means anything. Only in my disdain for mankind that my care and thought for people shine through. I love to hate people, but when I meet them I can't help but love them, care for them, give them the benefit of the doubt, etc. I hate how wonderful I am. I'm so free and trusting, so gullible. I can't let myself be used again. I won't fall into some trap of a relationship. I will have no one! Nothing! I will be free! But I don't need to be.

It is good to speak to people, to hear what they have to say, to hear what they think. All we really need to do is ask people questions. Difficult questions. I hate people who hide. Who hide in fear. Who hide from that which is right before their eyes in fear that it is genuinely there. We must fight against everything, confront everything, say everything. Even if we are wrong, even if it is false.... If we do not say it, let it out, then it will continue to be a little fear, a little possibility, a little truth in our fake lives. Live. Live and live. Live and live and live. Live and say. And speak. And let yourself fail to know by attempting to try.

My father is a mute.

I have the blood of a vampire running through my veins. I soar through the dark nights of the mind and take from whatever I can. I suck dry my victims and lavish myself in their blood. From them I can see the *reloin* and gurgle the waters that must be relished, like a relish, and taken in so that it can occur. I can then make the world my own, walk into the hall of mirrors and make the reflections all dim, green and gray, hear the whispering vibratos of the moon and let the goop train upon myself. And this in itself is grand. And this in itself is ecstatic.

All along I've been watching you, waiting for you, coming for you, and you to me. And now, soon enough, we will reach our peak. We will become, we will see, it will be there, we will see it, find it, know it, and have it.

I can hear the words now, it speaks to me, it gives me its name. It is alive. It is already here. It is already complete. It shares everything with me. The voice of it, this being, is my forever companion. And life is lit, and the fire burns bright even in the coldest winter.

It says, "do it, more, again, again," and I listen to it and trust in it. I put my faith into it and let it continue. For all things must continue, praise...!

The man that I killed was a murderer, a rapist, a pedophile, a disgusting waste of space upon the Earth. Why should I hide it? Why should I pretend to regret it? I have taken a life and now that is with me, forever. It gives me power. It taunts me. It drags me to a kind of madness. To take a life, it is a horrifying thing! Because it is so much! And then *you* are so much! And what else then can you be? What else then are you, but a killer? *That's what it is!* You are so much more than it! So much more than everything, so much more than nothing.

Do you sit quietly under the stars and gaze out? Do you hold yourself? What is the reason that you yell? We often only yell because we don't understand ourselves. Or, maybe we do? Maybe it's just proper manners....

I am a horrible rapist. I take what I want from men and women. I use them.
I suck them dry.

You fall apart. You fall away. You do not look and see what is there. You are blind; your eyes are clouded. When you speak it is garbled nonsense. When you cry you are there. When you sleep you are there. When you wake you fall away from it all again.

I have become a God, thank God. I suppose I always was a God. It is so light, so sweet, to be this way.... To have pure creation within me. To see and know all. I am with everything. I am emptied. Yes, to be emptied is a great pleasure. Nothing is sacred, for everything is.

All can be done. Nature can be remade, desecrated, and born again. Your body may be yours, yours to do whatever you will with it. And all the horrors can be overcome, yet remain.

You can remake your body. You can split it open and remove the insides. I have done this. I have peeled my skin from my chest and removed my limits. Search inside your mind and see that vast landscape without a body. You yourself are that landscape. The ocean washes over you...but again, what are you?

I have never faced abuse. I have never been maltreated. My parents have loved me and love me still. I am not sure how I will react when they die. They have named me the executor of their will because they trust me and know I handle things well. They taught me to be honest and to do what I wish with my life, but also to always be prepared, to have a plan, to take great care in your finances. And I believe in this, truly. They have taught me to take care of myself, to never accept treatment below what I deserve. And I have done it. I care for my lover. I hope to treat her well. She means so much to me. I could die, and still I would be happy.

Your words become meaningless. "I," "you," "here," "there," "etc." What else do you have? No body.

The words are spoken to communicate something, but nothing is understood, only more words are given which point away from what you wish to speak. What do you wish for? What do you know? Nothing, of course.

I have lived a thousand lifetimes. I am the reincarnation of a great spirit. I am destined for greatness, even if none know my name. I do not require love, nor fame. For I am the great one, even if it is only I that make it so. For I am a great thing, beyond the known or the unknown.

Christian McDonough

Your thoughts are not words, nor images, they are presences. What is that presence that you hold onto now? Where is it? Why is it? Did you ever stop to think about your thoughts? What do they mean to you?

And what do they mean to me? I listen to you. I listen to your thoughts, your presence, your presences. It just goes on and on. And two are there, mine and yours. In speaking of it now I can see it. Ours are together. And the body is gone, words are gone, yet I use them. If I could I would simply show it to you....Inside it, with you....

But that is a story for another time.

Know now all that you need to know. Knowing is simple. It is there. We are there with it, remember? Close your eyes with me and know it, whatever it is, and we will feel it. Sometimes that's all truth is, a little feeling, a pointless little feeling.... That is what we make of it. That is what we make it to be. There are no facts. There is no outside world. We are here, deep within.

Now we are with everything: with the plants, rocks, people, land, space, stars, everything. And we can feel for it. Just to feel, that's all we need. Do you like to feel it with me? The warmth of a body, of speaking tenderly, truthfully, exposed and vulnerable. It is all so sweet, yet so overwhelming, as if we had bodies that were shaking, shivering with excitement.

This sky before us is our sky: a great sky; a new sky. This land before us is a new land. What world will we make? What is the way it arose? What is the fundamental? Is it time? Space? Being? Consciousness? All these stupid things, what do they matter to us? We need new words, new ways, new thoughts, new meanings, everything born anew, again, aghast, away, awash, and willing...?

The pain. Pain that we feel. Suffering that we endure. It will still come. We can't avoid it. What pain have you faced? What pain have you felt? Did someone hurt you? Did someone speak to you? Did someone touch you? Did someone take something from you? Hurt someone you loved? Or did something simply happen? Did it all just seem to go away? And what were you left with? What do you have now? It will happen again. Big or small. But we will face it. We will stand tall! Haha! Look at me. Please, look at me. I love you. Don't worry. It will all be ok.

Do you speak to people? Do you ask them questions? Is there someone that you let it all out to? You need this! I need this! It does a lot just to say things. Sometimes I think I can't say something because it will be upsetting. But – at least, if you're not around shitfucks – there is always a way to say it that will not be upsetting, that will be okay. It can be okay. It's so scary. It's so hard. Sometimes it feels like there is a physical block preventing it from coming out, some shit piece of your soul which wants you to be trapped, which wants you to suffer. Do not give in to it! Fight against it! I promise, it will be alright!

If you would just get up and do something. Groom yourself, go outside, go for a walk.... I promise, you'd feel much better. That's how it works. We're really quite simple creatures. It's not that hard.

We have returned. The flames rise to meet us. Our hell, our heaven. The light is blinding. So much can be done here. The fantasy can be fulfilled.

Settle yourself. Be quiet. Be still. Did you know you could be so still, and that you could do so of your own will?

Yes, it is already here. And the angels, our own angels, their half-cocked faces and their green, molding mouths, are here to stay....

The dome broke open and the space was filled. You are there, comfortable and free, as the world itself is torn apart. You are the one who has torn it apart, who has made it as it must be. And you know what the meaning is. You know what was necessary. Come and laugh and look. Let the joke be played! It is for you! And I give it to you!

You live with me. You love with me. You know me and I know you. I had a life with you that you did not know. A life that was so beautiful, so perfect, so full. And it will always be there. It will always be here! within the book. I'm so happy...I'm so happy.... Tell me. Speak to me. Speak in whispers to the book, to its pages, and infuse within them your soul, as my paltry souls reside in it as well. And just think of all the books to come!

Do you love someone? Do you think you are meant to be together? Do you get upset when they look at others? Do you think they're against you, secretly? That they have dark thoughts against you that they will never share? And what about your thoughts? I'm sure there have been moments when you hated them, when you wished they would disappear, maybe even die. Maybe once or twice a wave of hate washed over you, and fear, and you hoped you'd never see them again, that they wouldn't walk through that door, smile, and embrace you.... Never again.

And do you care about your parents? Your family? Do they mean very much to you? Why? Or why not? You don't need them. They could hurt you! You might be better off, much better off, without them! Or maybe you need them. You couldn't live without them. Everything you do is in relation to your parents.

Your parents don't know you, because you are only all that they wished for, you are only all that they asked for. They don't know you; they know themselves. And no one could ever know who you are because you are no one, because that person who you are, who you could be, is dark, hidden within, not even yet born.

Sometimes I am "inspired," and then a little stream comes out and soon enough dries up, but I might attempt to dip my toe into it further.... But I find only mud. The stream dirtied, diluted, drained. Can you tap into your little streams? Do you? And what comes out!? You must let it come out! Why not? Why? Because it is you! Your little soul! Millions of little souls within you!

Together, we can overcome all, we can say anything and have it mean nothing. Therefore we are free to say everything and have it mean just as much. I do not believe in the power of words, of media.... Ultimately it means nothing to me. And because of this all is permissible in art. Have you ever allowed yourself to think this way? I used to try very hard, with lots of thought, to make it so that I allowed myself to think the most horrible things, to have those things which might commonly be labeled "intrusive thoughts" come through and pass by as though they were no different than any other. It is good to let these thoughts come and to welcome them, to see them through and let them go. Through this you can express anything. Don't you want to? You can say awful things. One of the most awful: I want to fuck my mother, *or*, I want to fuck my father. There, I said it. And I have thought it. This thought has passed my mind, this desire. And I let it go.

It means nothing to me.

How many "modes of thinking" will be contained within this book? Alone, fewer than I should like. But with you the possibilities are endless. Each sentence reinterpreted by you, reknown by you, reborn by you. And if, by some chance, I were to move you, to change you, the future might be bright for us. The future might hold us to its bosom and coddle us, comfort us. We might be children again, in a world full of bright, tender movement, in a world of bliss. Together.

What is it like for you, walking about the world? You move on, you sit, you work, what is it like? Is it a mindless thing? Do you have a sense of yourself as you go on? Please, consider how it must be for yourself in relation to others. Each has their own sense of the world, each is seeing it in another way, yet all experience it *as if* it were the only way! As if we all were ourselves, all were one. But, thank God, we are many. I see it and I can't see it, how it is, that is, how it is for me. So monotonous for me. Always this way or that until something shakes it up. Do you get shaken up? It is shaken up and then all is so different, interesting, great, or horrible. But for some this might be how it is always, and then it is really nothing, for them. But for you, what is it?

I am so sleepy. Are you? We can rest together now. And everything shall be calmed. And everything so sweet. Ahh....

God? Where is God? Oh! There! With you! What? What do you mean? What do you see? I see you, only you. All I need, you.

A massacre within you. I know it's true. I believe you. I know what happened. I was there with you. All that changed in those moments. All that began. All that ended.

Were you there with me when I went through it? All you have to say is "Yes."

You are so much. You have grown. You have changed. You can look up. You can open your eyes. You can do it! I believe in you!

Hahaha! I'm excited to show you what's next! This will be fun.

Are you ready? I have worked so hard to bring you here....

Don't turn away! Not yet! Not now!

Resurrection

The ultimate thing, all that I am, all that you are, and all that the world could be, could see, from within me, here and now.

Behold!

UNBECOMING

835

And no more was done.

Jump up and down
Love me
Love me

Don't you know?
Clown
Clown

The end never retracts itself –
Your worries only protract their self.
Ply the pussy apart,

Maggot fucked

There, Was, Air, Where
Simply, like sand –
Silt. Shake, Shake. And,
It opens up, and look inside.
See the sights which sought
You. Hairy, Bald, knobbles.
Snickelodeon Snakeskin...

Singing, Singing
Tear the Tear, cut
And cut, and cut,
Steel – Golden Reels
Killing and Culling
Chrysanthemummis,
Red, Bleeding,
            Huu' Muus.

Horrible, Dying
What shines?
What's dim?
(*A tragedy.*)

Insanity. Reality. Creatures. And night. Fighting. Living. Roaring. To life. Massive. Meaning. Making. Free. Jesus! Christ! Under. The tree. Blasphemy. Blackening. Roasting. The pyre. The mire. The mystery. The mystic. Unchained. Unlived. Undone. Unknown. Away. Awash. Again. Alone.

It will be something else. It won't be this or that. It will be something that can't be said.

Unbecoming

I don't know. I don't know what I'll say. I don't know what I'll do.

He doesn't know. He doesn't know what he'll say. He doesn't know what he'll do.

She doesn't know. She doesn't know what she'll say. She doesn't know what she'll do.

They don't know. They don't know what they'll say. They don't know what they'll do. All of them. Look, all of them! There! And what are they doing? And what is happening? And what is here?

A life is lived only for pleasure, only for fun,
But also for meaning, for truth, for justice
And also for purpose and presence and lies.
To make everyone, everything, a surprise....
And the ever-golden compass doth turn
And point and poke to a new land,
A new land of thought,
And of great, bright things bought
For you to hide and hide.

Dying, you present yourself
Here, as if all is
As it should be
And completely sure. Don't you
Recognize how it is?
As this is The Horse-House.

Dying, did you see
How Jengika looked
At you, as you
Begged and Groveled?

Unbecoming

847

It can become
All that it was
Before and again
Never wanted or undone
And I will hold you
And you will hold me?
(Of life born anew.)

And behold
It is seen.

The Answer! The Answer given! Given to you!
Yes, only for you, for you are the one that sees it!
You see it here, in between and within!
You see it there, from my hand, it seems to bend...
And blend...and fade away...and Rise!!

Oh, to rise and rise, that is the answer!
And, oh, to see and see, that is the answer!
Oh, and, oh, to be, and to be, and forever and on!

Again! Again! Let us say it again!
Let us do it again!
A thousand more poems!
A thousand more Answers!

And then, and then, the Ends!

A song to sing!
For you and I!
A day to dream!
For you and I!
A philosophy to speak!
To the Gods who weep,
For they do not know,
Do not,
And never have,
Known why.

Don't you cry…!
Don't you cry…!
Because I'm here
And you know why.

Don't you cry…!
Don't you pout…!
You know I'm always
Looking out.

Entrapment! Entrapment! You made me say it! You made me say all these things! Your fault! It's all your fault!

I didn't do nothing!
I didn't mean nothing!
I lied about all things!
I have become all

Nothing Nothing!
All nothing!
That's what I want!
And that's what I am!

I did not say I was a killer. Nor a rapist. Nor an assailant!
Only a victim! Only a victim! I am always forever

ONLY A VICTIM.

And so much more! I can do anything. I can do everything. Haha. You hate me? You love me? All will love me soon enough. None will know. None will see. Only him or she. Or another or another. I don't know. I don't know why not. I don't know why so? Who? And where? And when!?

Again.
Again.
Again.
Again.

And she deserves to die. She deserves it. She did this to me. She murdered me. She raped me. She took everything from me. And he deserves to die for thinking these things about me. How could he? He was supposed to be everything to me. He was supposed to care for me, to be with me.

Don't you see?
Don't you know?

This will not end well. I will cut her throat. I will remove her limbs. I will murderfuck her. I will eviscerate her. All she is. All she cares for. It will all go quite badly.

In the mountains there is a beast. Its red eyes peer out from its cave. It heaves forth, slowly, each step echoing, a hard plod, weathered by the fur. Its fangs deep, vicious, and real. Its bite ready to kill.

And can't you leave me? Can't you leave me alone? I can't believe it. I was right and he told me I was wrong. No, really. It's a horrible feeling. To feel that way. To know you're right but they all treat you like a fool. They laugh at you. I can't stand it. I'd kill myself. I'd kill myself just to spite them. To rub it in their faces. Who's wrong now? Who's hurting now? Who will live to suffer!? Not me! Not me! Not me!

And she.... I want her to take me. I want her to take me away. I don't need it. I don't need to stay. I will walk, walk, far and away. And never meander, never not ever, never again, never leave. Not now, not known. Under the stone. I try to stand. I am there. I am trapped. I will never be free.

It comes and comes and comes to me....

And what was it?
And who?

Entombed within a great purpose, a sarcophagus of lies and deceit. Yes, that is a purpose too, some might not think it, nor know it, but to them it is true. That there lives an old fogey who has traits most foul. That becomes and beguiles upon and with the young Miles.
Who doth know what ith coming, yeth coming forth with
The traitor, you traitor! I could only take a pith.

THE POET! THE ARTIST! THE BLUBBERING FOOL!

how quiet...how cruel...they treat me like a tool....

And this is how it is all seen, for within such a septum the senses of the mind deceive, misinterpret, and finagle, just by behaving as they are intended to do.

And it lives again! It breathes! It SEETHES!

And what was it that the princess said? "I am so delicate, I am to be preeeened!"

A thousand more, a thousand less. Nothing stopped, all undressed.

855

The tall!
The tear!
I love you, I fear....

My dear, don't you know?
I am a shoe. I am a show....

A triumph! A triumph! Yes! This is what it all has been!
A disaster! A master! A meiser for Shane!
You are all apart and nothing and falling, and don't know nor see a thing!
A miserable ROT! A horrible LOT!

The Pattern Puffs Againe!
The Monster ROARS for shame!

You do not see...You do not know...
For don't you recall...?
I TOLD YOU SO!!!!!

A trap of a trap of a trap. You're trapped! The butt flopped up and down and jiggled and swayed. No one heard, no one stayed.

We see things...
And we think things...
And we even see that we think things...

But what would we see?
What would we think?
With the possibility
For a man
And, or, a woman
To fly
To die
And live again

To croon
And cry
And become the moon

What would it be?
What would it be?

To be
To be

That which we are not
What one might not see
And then know
And know
And...

825

I am amazed to know
What it is that you hold
Within that small hand

A promised land

And the intricacies of life
What is wrong and what is right?

Do you have a monster, an animal, a scholar?
Within or behind
Your ever-growing mind?

How beautiful you are
And how delicate all you see

You must know

A million infinities

I have seen what was there
But please, forget me
I am not even here
I was never even there

A carcass crashed
Upon the land
And begun the life
Of the water and the sand

Who stood and watched
As all was said

Don't you know?
You're as good as dead.

826

Reach out for the youth, the youth that ties and binds
Numb the riot with the Novocain, it's there and ready
Consume a quail, as is told in the scripture
And hunger, yes, hunger, for the forthcoming claim

I will tell it!
       That is what he said, for from high upon
The mount he'd mounted
       He saw what he wanted
And spoke as he saw

Yes! This will be it! You see the crack?
       For there was a great crack,
       A great cackle too,
For upon that wall
Upon that mountain
It was true

Young turtle doth come
And made frigid it stood
Not moving
Not speaking
Only being as it could

Pluck me, shuck me
Make me into your meat
Murder and foul play
Are my tastiest treats

The End is here. The End has ended. You did it, didn't you?
You saw what you needed to see. You read what you needed to read.
Even if it was only seen for a second, it was up to you to grab onto it
To take it and make it yours
Make it known
Make it real

And you must do so!
You must make it so!
Back! Go back and see it again!
And end. End. End.

The triangular function of the great consumption
How you tried and then found
What it was you were looking for!
I am so proud, oh so proud, of you!

And look! Look, fool! Don't go away! Don't fall away!
Stay and stay and stay and stay. Don't let it sway,
Don't let it linger...Make it and make it and stay and play.

And again! Rise up! Rise up and hold the bay! Back
From the bend! And, sure, pretend,
But don't go on with a lie
And don't cower and cry

I speak to you
I coddle you
I raised you with grace

Now please go and live
Life, embrace!

<h1 style="text-align:center">829</h1>

Everything you did
Everything you thought
Was oh so beautiful
Was filled to the naught...!

I missed you, I'll miss you, I miss you again
Please, don't forget me, know that I am your friend.

And I care for you
            (And fallen apart again.)
And I love you
And I miss you
And I want you

And a trial was a trial
And you with your End
And your Answer
And your freedom

Yes, play! Pretend!
And game! And joke!

Even let yourself choke.

For you were such a blessing to me
For you were such a comfort

I couldn't ask for more
But then again I couldn't ask for less

I am happy to have known you
I am happy that I guessed

Vipers come at me, at us. And they reach for us. They reach for our mouths; they want to kiss us. They're so sexy! Oh my! I'm surprised that they're sexy, just look at their eyes....

They come and come and freak us good.... Oh wow, oh no, this is rape, yet it should....

Be something more, something real, through the door, through the window, through the gate.... The symbol of a great hate. For when it is unleashed, for when it is here? Or there, with you? There will be great fear. For with all things come a wave of hate. For with all things there are horrible dates, nights, frights, and fights.... For without any champion the masturbators are right.

They live as they should. They live as they need. To take pleasure in everything? To take pleasure? To heed? To heed it all as it is. To become what we must. And be and become, oh fuck, I'm gonna come.

But the young fart didn't see it. And was soon decapitated. I couldn't look. Later, I masturbated. Hung on the wire. Was the body of the bitch. A little dachshund. God, it was rich. How the freaks gagged it. And massacres again. For life in this land. Is always for sin.

Hundred, thousand, million, or more. A rattle of death. The cow made his score.

Achoo. Bless you. I was later regurgitated. And recreated through the womb. As a virgin falcon mated.

Misery made me into who I am. I love to suffer. No, I need to suffer. It is necessary for me to be this way, for me to be able to do the things that I do. If I didn't suffer I wouldn't be anything. I'd be just like the rest of you.

Don't you know that?
It's true.
But not really.
How so?
Beauty
It holds you
And supports you
It's true!
No,
Not really.

And the magnificence of life is my greatest inspiration. It's all I need. It's all anyone needs, really. No food, no water, no bread, none dead. A mite and a worm begin to butt heads. Ahhhhhh.... There is a well to dip into. To fall into. To die. This well, once tapped into, is brilliant and sublime.

The songs they sing!
How elegant, how grand,
Such beauty in their hands.

The music of Klezmer
Is divine and true.

I trapped the souls
Of all kinds of frogs

And made them croak
If only for me.

Incorrigible thoughts,
Leave me now!

Let me go!
Leave me be, anyhow! Anyway! Any style! I could write like this for days.
The miners are crying. Out for their stays. Undangerous, unhaggardly.
Unlifed ungain.
Words make a mockery, a malady, of men.

Christian McDonough

How does the river run? How does the boat shake? How does anything, everything, make? Uhhnnn.... I cracked open my skull. But still no answer, look at this, all null.
A miserable pile of putrid stench.
A disgusting howl made into a mensch.

The roar was too loud. It hurt my ears. It made me sad. And how come when I'm sad there are others who are happy? And how come when I cry, not everyone cries too?

I was laid to rest, there, under the stool
And above the door, on the sign, it read:

Here he lies, the ol' chap who is dead.

And the barkeep whistled
And cleaned up his glass.
And all the pretty ladies did look about with sass.
More joined in, all looking about,
Even the older, even with gout.

A master I need. To teach me what is what. I need something more. Something less. Something, but. But I need to have a life. Oh, yes. I almost forgot. I need to have a life. Where I do something meaningful and with others. Not to just constantly be alone and away from everyone and everything.

Yes! I'll fight in the war! What war? Any war, it doesn't matter. And any side that'll take me. I'll do my best, yes, it's no matter.

A life is lived for the benefit of one or many. What will you choose? What will you hold? Are you there? Are you listening?

The growth is a measure of the amount of death one can withstand. A total death is a beginning, and an end is a reaching for trials. For miniscule moments. For something else, something new. If one sees the action as a fundamental piece of their becoming they might then take the stance that their "oddity" is their greatest aspect. And do they have access to the sublime? The limitless? Where have they placed their limits? At what point? A point beyond their own consciousness? For this is where one should always place it. For only then may one achieve it.

The world is round. The sky is blue. There are things called clouds. There are people, like me and you. People speak. People live their own lives. They wear clothes. They marry. They do all kinds of things. And there are animals. One that I like is the skink. And there are insects. One that I like is the praying mantis.

I scratch my elbow. I look at my elbow, the skin, and then scratch the skin. The skin of my elbow, for it was itchy. It had an itch. It was itching. And I took my hand, made it into something like a paw or a claw, my fingers all together, and I scratched it. I scratched my elbow. I scratched my itchy elbow because it was itchy, because it needed to be scratched and so was scratched with my hand, with my fingernails. And the fingers all together in the shape of something like a claw, or maybe a paw – no – more a claw than a paw.

We must say things like "hello!" and "good morning!" whenever we can. We must be polite and friendly. But we must also be able to do the opposite. *(Still, it was good to see you.)* We must protect ourselves, for people will always take what they can from you. People like that know how to spot a potential victim. But they should behave like us. We should also overthrow the government, but subtly, by refusing to purchase all products and being self- reliant and independent, or, at least, independent from corporations. And what would happen then? It might be interesting.

Anyway, we must speak. What must we say when someone asks us a question? The truth, as best we can, but made appropriate for the situation. We must learn and understand social cues, even if it's difficult. And question yourself, your language, constantly. Always try to be as accurate as you can, even if only in your head. You can correct what you said in your head if you were unable to say it in person, maybe they left before you had a chance to correct or you didn't yet have the courage (you'll need to develop that), so correct it in your head. If you continue to do this it will become easier to be truthful (or perhaps we should say honest?) in the moment.

What is to be believed? No value. No sense. No way to govern or control. We must be rigorously self-controlled yet be beyond control. We must fight and kill. We must be killers and therefore be beyond control. Beyond victimhood. Beyond accusation. Beyond sense. Beyond understanding. Maybe, maybe not. No value, and all can be done. No judgment, and all can be made. The political is ultimately creative. We must be true creatives (or just me) and create without limits, without fear, continuously create, and quickly, and well. I can do it. I'll do it for you if you're too chicken! I dare you! Come on! I dare you to do it!

841

A manufactured sense of meaning through continuous mental effort: thought, development, interaction, etc. From this a new self can be made. One simply needs to study all that they do, their self, and keep good track of it, maybe write it down, then counter it as best you can. Do this for a time, develop it, make a habit of it, then again study what you do, your habits, write it down, etc., and counter it yet again. Continue this indefinitely and you should be a genius soon enough.

A malingerer! A malingerer! A filthy, dirty deceiver! You do bad things! You think bad thoughts! And your life should end! Your life should end! You are evil! Pure evil! For we have made it so! We have made it so and so it is! Yes! Yes! It is! And end yourself now. Go ahead, please do so....

And truth...! My tender friend...! I was with you!!! I loved you to the end!!!!
We have become, and become and become.... All that we needed...! All that
we cared for...!! All that we asked for...!!! And So Much More!!!!

The Real attained through continuous self-subjugation is only a single offshoot of its many possibilities. For the Real when fully realized, when made to be as it must be, as it necessarily *will* be, is indefinable, could be compared to McDonough's Something, if you like, and is always there, and: *because it is indefinable it is therefore unattainable.*

If God exists, It is now with us, and we can channel It, be It, and manipulate It. Like God, morality is a rotting carcass which we play with and poke at for our own ends. God is a special kind of carcass though and still fills us with hope as we dance dressed in Its remains. Morality's remains, however, stink too badly, and so we only shove this carcass into the face of others to remind them of their past deeds, making sure to keep as much distance from it as we can.

The body itself, every body, is a labyrinth without end: an individual is always lost in the body. The body can be known as a whole or as made up of individual parts. Still, each body remains unknown and the body itself is also lost in relation to everything.

The apocalypse is already here, though it is very slow and thoughtful. It is considerate and allows us the smooth transition to a post-apocalyptic state. This may have something to do with capitalism.

The world is fundamentally unfinished. That is, it is being created as we go along. This means that we, as well as everything else, contribute to its continued creation. Just think, hasn't everything changed so much? All of our thoughts are radically different than they were just a hundred years ago. If everything in the world progresses, changes, does the world itself not then do the same? This means we have a moral obligation to the world. We could even think of the world as our collective child. In fact, I think we should! How would you treat a child? Actually, that's a bad question. There are so many horrible parents out there. Alright. You need to consider how everything you do influences a child, every act they see, everything they hear you say. Each event has a large impact on it (the child). But with so many people the world is subject to all kinds of influence. First of all I think we should get rid of the media, specifically digital social media, that's what I mean when I say the media. *(And no.)* They're not helpful, they're very influential, and they are changing the world (the media). I don't like how they are changing the world. I'm sure there could be some media that is doing something positive, but it's not worth it to me. Of course, you can disagree. *(And who else is there?)* But let's just say we'll get rid of it for now. Now things are much simpler. We need to be kind to each other, reach out to one another, and focus on forming connections in the world. I realize getting rid of "the media" has made this a lot more difficult, but that's the point. It needs to be difficult. It needs to induce some level of anxiety because in these cases when that anxiety is overcome a genuine catharsis is realized. *(Another.)* I could go into more detail but I don't want to. So now we reach out to each other, we are kind, etc., and we work on our projects. That's it. The rest is suggested throughout the book, look and you'll see.

It wasn't the way they described it. It wasn't anything they knew.

I will continue. As I always have. To be with it, that moment where The Detective finally found all that he searched for, for he is only a detective due to his great desire to know! And know what? That is the question. Haha! It was in that moment that he saw a great eye, each miniscule vein bubbling with blood to power its processes.... And The Detective then reflected upon his own processes, his sight, his thought, his smell.... How he teased and taunted to take from those he spoke with, to take from them all...how he confronted them, challenged them.... Was this not what now happened to him, before it all? The beam within the pupil of the eye shot forth, blew his hair back, fucked him in a sense. And his own eyes, the pupils, reflected the beam back upon itself. Yes....A relationship....A dependent relationship.... For it could only be that Mystery if he were to search for it, to not know it, and therefore to supply it with its covering, with its content, its structure.... The structure was then revealed to him. A giant, perfect diamond...yet imperfect, as it moved between even and uneven, as each face grew and shrank in accordance with the other, yet not even so! They seemed to grow beyond each other, beyond their own limits. Of course, yes, of course, for such limits were abstractions as well.... All an abstraction for him, The Detective, to crack, to shape, and to narrativize.... That silly narrative which he was caught within....The Old Detective's Tale.... He laughed again, he smiled again, he thought he might never smile again, not after what happened.... And it was!

Nothing! Forever nothing and nothing no more! I can kill you again and call you a whore!

"I told you, she said she never wanted to see you again and she didn't want to talk about it anymore. Then she ran off," said Gulliver.

The teetering off the overground faucet.... How the phone rang forever and ever! And mother never said no more! Beyond her grave! Beyond that door!

"But what about the rest of it? There was a whole box of dynamite in the closet," said Franklin.

A miserable cunt. A watering hole...! All along the shore the crabs danced and dangled before them. They didn't seem to know what was soon enough coming, yes, soone enoughe couminge!

"I cannot speak no more. The whore is at the door. The bleeder is running out. The bats are coming out." And it was spoken ever so softly yet screamed forever more. And there were a million busting through – none could hold them back, not anymore....

A whistle. I whistled. I whistled and thought. And knew. And it was there. Some whole song. For me to sing to you. For you to hear. And it was heard. You just heard it, for you thought it just there. And by God, what a moment! What a thing – to be feared!

A minister came up and spoke, he said that the devil was inside of him and that he must be killed. He smiled then and waited for someone to do it.

A miserable man walked into my hand, and worded it so perfectly,
He said, "You better run; I'm not having fun. I've come to kill you, cordially."

A flat land. The wind blowing through the bushes. The bushes big, overgrown. The yellow sun clouded. The clouds clouding. The yankees yodeling. A perfect day. And Jumper comes in, the mongrel. Barks. Drools. Slobbers. Says, "I am not a dog. I am a human being." Dog comes in, laughs. Jumper goes to the cliff to die. Doesn't. Moves along. Cries. Woman, named Woman, comes. Fucks Jumper, who's not a dog. Then leaves. Woman grows up. Was very young before (unknown to Jumper (Jumper is dumb)). Grows up and kills Andy Warhol before Solanas attempts. Odd time problem. Jumper jumps on a naturally made trampoline in the forest. A thousand eyes all look and see and know that another person (a man named Gromlin) is alive and well in Southern California. Gromlin goes on with his life, wonders about some things, and eventually dies. I...

A fly on the wall, listening. A maggot in the ball, glistening.

If you are here with me please note it. Everything happens again. And trials weave in and out and around all from the great googly eyes of the dream. The dream which holds you. Poor prude, you don't know. For the grain is wed with the redness of blood. Which, this blood, it pours from your veins as they, split open, let out to become remains. Under the red ivory that has become your skin – you foul temptress – lived your life of sin. How now? What now? Do you have no shame?

No, don't get me wrong. I don't mean anything by it. It is only that which is necessary. Think of all the work we've put in, together, for this precise moment. How queer it all is now. How unnerving, how empty. But still, so full. Judge me not, lest ye be judged. Yet I don't care. Pour away. Pour away, poor fool. Poor fool. Poor fool. Hang the red guard. Fuck the cheap shit. You are a bastard, who is your mother? You are a bastard, who is your father? The gangrene comes again. Fly away. I'm so empty. I'm so empty. I'm so empty. I'm so sad. But I am so happy. And you should be too. Holler again, holler again!

I already did take it.

An inquest will now be considered. For what you have done there will be no reprieve from such a state. Yes, it shall continue on. Do you know your friends? They are not yours anymore. We have taken them. Do you know your life? We have changed it; you do not know it anymore. Do you fear death? Worry not, it will never come. Let it go on without you. Let it get away from you. You don't have to think anymore. It'll all be taken care of. Why did you ever think? You're so silly.

Vanquish them. Finish them off. Take them away. Run. Run now. Grab your coat. It's cold. Don't let it get to you. You'll find a place soon enough. You're bleeding. Get a rag. Hurry. Hurry. Try for something else, why don't you? Something new. New again.

They did it again. Oh no. You fell for it.

You are in touch with the totality of it all. You have no thoughts, no sensations, no feelings. Everything simply *is* – and you are within it. Enacted by it, living it. You are *lived through*. The boundless reality, the reality you hold in your hands, is in fact yours! Everything is foreign to you because you feel it all. It is so much that you cannot contain it. You do not let it limit you. You are not limited. You are eternal. You do not let yourself be limited. The body is nearly forgotten. A power grows within you. A bliss is felt eternally. A moment is protracted beyond time itself. But these statements still occur to you: "I'm worthless. I hate myself. I'm ugly. I'm stupid. No one cares about me. I'm not worth caring about. I don't know who I am. I don't want to think about anything. I want to go away. I want to kill myself. I want to cut my head off. I want to slit my wrists. I want to blow my brains out. I want to be a different person, a person who isn't hated, who isn't bad, who isn't weak, who isn't always crying. A person who has real emotions. Everything I do is fake. I'm always putting on a show. I just want attention. I scream and cry so people will talk to me. So people will look at me. I'm the only one who is important. They don't understand me. They're too stupid. They're against me. They pretend they don't understand. They're pretending they don't know what's wrong. It's obvious. But they act like it's not. They just act stupid. But they know they can help me. They just want me to suffer. I know everything. *I* am everything. No one knows the things I know. I am the first of my kind. I will show them all how much better I am than them. They will know *my* name."

The greatest one. The perfect one. The masterly might of all that I have done. And you, give it to me, let me have it for a moment. I reach up and see! I see and I feel! I feel and I know! The rain fell like dewdrops on grass (meaning it did not fall), but each falling, each falling moment, each seemed to bleed out on to the sight, to crack through some glass. It was all there and against the skyline where great, massive, empty and horrid buildings stood, where trees paled in comparison to all that man had made. And people's lives made horrid! Horrid yet beautiful! More full than ever! More powerful than ever! Through all that we have done. Yes, think of all those great minds and all that they have done for us. Now we can make ourselves into anything, all it takes is time. And money. But good, why not? We all want money. We want what we want and we wait for it to be given to us. And the shoes, the feet, walking down the street. Each one its own step. Each step its own gait. Some waddle. Some tiptoe. Some stomp. Some gallop! Each with their own, and their thoughts! Their thoughts! What should I wear? What will I do? I can't believe I lied. I can't believe I'm going to die. And more and more, more than one can put to words. All so beautiful, cursed, and absurd.

Untrained and unlearned. The bastard was reborn. I missed you and I'll hold you.

I don't think that fighting is very good for you. You'll get hurt.
Trust me, I do it all the time. And to fight is essential. If you don't fight you can't withstand what will come. For in life all types of things will come. You have to fight throughout life.
But no, you have a choice to fight.
Yes. And if you decide not to, you'll die.
No.
Yes. If you're not fighting, you're dead. You have to fight every day. For everything. It's unavoidable. It really is. We're all animals.
I am not an animal.
Then you're a fool.

I hate artists. I hate musicians too. They are dirty little fools living in filth. It's true. I'm not joking.

Every artist is an idiot, and must be so, for with all they do...? And all they say...?

How treacherous it was to feel the green beneath the steam. I am always sad. I am always lonely. And what about you?

Please, do not leave me. I did it all for you! I tried so hard! I tried so hard! And what? What? This is the thanks I get? A passing glance? A little stare? I did everything for you! And you throw me to the side like a piece of trash? Like shit? I should fucking kill you! You fucking deserve it, you dumb fucking bitch! You filthy cunt! I fucking hate you!

But this is only a taste, only a wee testament to my newfound grace, to my belligerent mind which runs all the time.........!

Untangle this knot of your life. Fall away, far away, from the mess. Look back on it, intensely, but keep yourself hidden. Do you see it...? There, I see a desire that you've kept hidden. Let it out in some way, maybe write it in a journal. And there, I see a problem with a family member. You should try to talk to them about it. It's too important to let it go completely unaddressed. I have done this too. It might not change anything but it's good to be able to do it. And there, you wonder why you have trouble with friends. Find better friends or correct your personality. No, don't be so sentimental. That's not who you are inherently, that's just you being an asshole. Anyway, I have to go, you carry on with this....

Why? Why did I say that? Why do I say this? What is the point of any of it? What is the point of any of it? What is the point of any of it? Those last three sentences should be read with completely different intonations, if you catch my drift…. Don't you know everything? Don't you know what I'm thinking, what I want from you, at every moment? No? Well then, there must be something wrong with you, I'm sure….

What is happening to you? What is happening to you right now? What is going on in there? You feel it, don't you? Yes, I'm sure you do.... How good, how good that you feel it....

A barbecue that I had once with my family. My father burned the meat.

Intestinal damage occurs when too much sodium is taken in. The pope should be killed. I'm not joking. He is requiring all priests to engage in pedophilic acts in the name of The Lord. The storm is coming, you should go outside and wait for it. It will be nice and good. I'm happy to see things are continuing. I wake up every day and smile. It is easy to get out of bed. The planets turn, the stars align as well, and Malorothus is raised up from the dead!

Leit is there too and he kisses you. He likes how things are. He likes to see your dread. Leit and Malorothus are my greatest creations. You don't even know them, yet they know you.

They know you so well. They think that you're swell. You are going to die a horrible death. I have seen it. It will be awful, terrible, disgusting and depraved. Even if only from reading this, it is true. And soon a plague will come and tear the lands down, away, and nothing new will be seen, known, or heard. A waterfall from the sky to flood all at once. And a face through it all, watching: *that is The Witness*. The Witness watches and is really just a concept, a construct, for a little thought experiment. For if we have a Witness, one that sees all and that, theoretically then, all is done for, then there is an easy way to attribute meaning to everything. The Witness sees it all and does it all – no, we do it all, but The Witness does it by seeing it, processing it, like it is all a great big film. And it is, isn't it?

Yes, it is. It is a great big little stupidity. Like that movie. Yes, all like that movie. And also a play. Oh, but such a tiny audience. And there is The Great Androgyne. A little biscuit of a woman! It's just because she's so sexy. And then Acephalous, the Headless Woman. She came to me in a dream. That dream really did occur. She really did say those things to me, my mother too. What did it mean? It moved me. Now it is with you. Who am I? Why do I have a name?

Christian McDonough? Harriet Grontly? Maestro Hilario? Munster Jocko? A Trolloper? A Golloper? A Magnificent Stew? These are all names, my names. And you?

Words were spoken, words were told. The carcass was covered in mold. And now all cleaned. And now all known. And all spoken to be spoken. This was pure life. This was pure triumph. The trial was overcome. Freedom was seen and thrown away. I lived again. I lived today.

And what else was there for you? And what more could be done?
I laughed, I laughed, I had so much fun.

Did you laugh? Did you cry? Was there anything more than that?

I am empty, I am speechless, but none of this is on track.

Day

LEIT: Mannerisms which occur in certain instances have had strong effects on me. Sometimes I see a person make a funny face and I realize how truly it is that they are and that they are within themselves. Separate from me. But their faces cripple into me and we are crippled together, as images.

MALOROTHUS: My ear is hurting, along with my head. Pain is a signifier of Rebirth.
I am in tremendous pain at the moment.

LEIT: I feel quite reserved, as if I've fallen into myself.

MALOROTHUS: Pain grows. Little droplets of pain flowering out of the sand and water. My head, what if it fell off?
Then, I would be a ligament of pain. My head would be replaced with Pain, "P-A-I-N" in big, bold letters.

LEIT: You are making a face.

MALOROTHUS: This project of mine which I have embarked upon, it is growing beyond myself. I work on it, bringing pain, and I cannot hold myself back from it. My ears feel so warm. I work on it, and it is as if I am not doing anything. I then feel quite reserved, as if I've fallen into myself.

LEIT: I have felt that way before, many times.

MALOROTHUS: What is it that you are talking about?

LEIT: The Perspective which has currently overtaken me, a sense of the totality of moments. I sometimes feel that I can understand everything completely inside of individuals and therefore inside of the universe. I've been pushing myself to be with others and it is coming along easier than ever.

MALOROTHUS: That's interesting.

LEIT: I am not speaking of myself.

MALOROTHUS: Separation from pain seems to come too easily. This falling into myself allows me to push the pain aside and then I hide in darkness. Darkness allows rebirth. Thank God, my ears are still hurting.

LEIT: Everything is moving so quickly. Everything changes in an instant. There is much more to time as it passes through my mind. How much time has elapsed since we've been here?
It feels like years, as if I had grown.

MALOROTHUS: Realizations, when they really come, are strong. They are like shifts within me. Sometimes it is like there is a very clear architecture of the "Soul." Does my "Soul" burn?

LEIT: The soul? I wondered about that for a very long time; I had no clear way to know it.

MALOROTHUS: And now?

LEIT: The soul is the fundamental basis of the Individual. It is what moves you, your own First Mover or Fundamental Cause. I think it has much to do with the personality as well.

MALOROTHUS: I don't really believe in the soul. The soul is only what gives us life. I see no need for a distinction between life itself and the soul.
The walls will all break down and my head will fall off. With my pain and rebirth I will not have a soul. I will continue. It is good to feel pain: I know I am alive.

LEIT: What else is there?

MALOROTHUS: Oh, look....

LEIT: There is light and there is peace

and there is that which is Whole and that which is Empty.

MALOROTHUS: And what of women? And men?

LEIT: There IS man and there IS woman and there is creation and objects and their paths....

MALOROTHUS: The object is supreme to the soul. I will burn up and shift and fall into myself and the object "IS" complete.

LEIT: Look. How you run your hand through your hair, Malorothus. And you just barely touched your ear. It is red.

MALOROTHUS: I make sure I am composed and I look directly ahead and I grace my ear with the tip of a finger only so that I may feel the pain and I endure it.
The sun is burning my eyes. It isn't pure, it's red like blood.

LEIT: What does it mean to bleed?

MALOROTHUS: My project will never come to be complete, will it? I will continue on and on until my head really does fall off. An image, the severed head held in one's own hands. The head's hands, and the head holds itself. A man lives without his head. Bleeding from it, there is a blessing in that. There is a meaning within the head.

LEIT: When I am separate and empty, in darkness. I hold my head in my hands. I cry. I cannot hide from my tears. I am sad.

MALOROTHUS: What are you sad about?

LEIT: I am sad because I am completely alone.

MALOROTHUS: As am I.

Incorrigible how – undefinable me – unforgettable you! And why and how and when and wherefore...? These questions they all come tumbling tumbling tumbling out the door.... Forsooth, wash bin, under...the skin...! I crapped in my pants! I shat on the dance.... The floor made a mess.... This is my manifesto! I contest!!!

Here. You should be able to save a life, to be thoughtful, caring, kind, and compassionate, to be helpful, understanding, etc., but you should also be able to literally murder someone. To kill someone in cold blood, maybe even for no reason. I'm not saying you should do it. But you should be able to. If you start thinking along these lines when developing yourself you'll become an amazing person. Why shouldn't you *be able* to do everything? This gives you strength, power, self-esteem, etc. So, do it. And then you can choose to be however you wish: nice, mean, thoughtful, smart, whatever, maybe, else, and?

I have finally attained supreme enlightenment. You are finished. I am done with you. I do not need you anymore. You were my tool, nothing more. Yes, I have betrayed you. But don't worry. I'm sure it will be nothing more than a joke to you, you little bitch. You little mongrel.

And suddenly you're back to being yourself again. You're alone again. You're crying again. Your body disgusts you again. There's nowhere to turn to, is there? But it always recurs. It becomes a joke, a game. Cycling between nothing and everything, between being yourself and being the world. You tease yourself, you fuck into others, becoming them and consuming them. You take their bodies as if they're your own. You tear your own body apart by fucking them. You fuck everyone. You fuck yourself. You fuck nothing. Do you know who you are then? You know nothing. You know nothing because you wish to be nothing, because you wish to be something else, but still *something*, not everything. You deny the reality of the emotions. You sever all connection, yet yearn for it, acting on this yearning, all the while telling yourself it is impossible, therefore making it impossible.

A thousand ends. A thousand questions. A thousand answers. A thousand lives. A thousand deaths. A thousand thoughts. A thousand ghosts. A thousand animals. A thousand people. A thousand births. A thousand miles. A thousand tortures. A thousand smiles. A man and a woman and a bird and a plan. And that was all it took to make me this man.

Day's end

LEIT: I have come again, as if back from the dead. I stand here risen up from the ground, covered in all kinds of Dirt. My hands are fragile. I am emaciated. My bones are cracking. What say you, "Balorothus?"

MALOROTHUS: I am standing like a statue, like Stone.

LEIT: I see him there, standing. How deranged that I can still see after it all.... I am completely blind.

MALOROTHUS: Like stone, I feel nothing and I am impenetrable by human hand, only a great force could melt me down and change me. It is the day's end, the sun is not yet fallen but it is falling, not risen any longer. The light is fading and so it seems to be burning more than ever as simple fire, not as the great flame of the sun.

LEIT: How queer it is at this time. My hands close. I can see in the distance a great thing coming towards us, a great, great thing.

MALOROTHUS: We shall be dirt together, as it appears that you once were.

LEIT: The light hurts my eyes. I should like to cover my eyes and look away forever. In turning away from this light I should emaciate myself further.

MALOROTHUS: Total totality of a designated form. Could something be totally one thing? It's too abstract.

LEIT: Upon complete emaciation and in death I should be more myself than ever before, a rotten twig. A rotten twig: I am all torn up.

MALOROTHUS: Train yourself to sense the others that are all here with us now. Listen to them....

LEIT: It is as if I am a child again, in a way....

MALOROTHUS: Some giant abstract rabbit weavles at us with its snout. Hopping only slightly to turn and look at us, but not at us, look and gaze over us.

LEIT: My mother was dear to me; I haven't seen her in years.

MALOROTHUS: Rabbits, like this one, are extremely distant from you and me.

LEIT: I'm so tired, again.

MALOROTHUS: It is falling apart, again.
My stone is cracking and now there are several pieces that are me.
Are you listening, Leit?

LEIT: There is a giant abstract rabbit or bunny and there is also a fox.
I am still covered in dirt. My face is contorted. At the moment I am feeling something, like how the fox completely ravages the bunny.... I mean rabbit.

MALOROTHUS: Oh God, one and one, alike as another.

LEIT: My fate was sealed years ago when he continued with his project.

MALOROTHUS: It is as if, as a stone, the feelings only wash over you and nothing comes through you.

LEIT: Until at once you are completely obliterated and torn apart from the inside out....
And I should add that the force which tears is itself a thing of a good and purely good will.

MALOROTHUS: I should fall silent but the hordes will not cease, all of them crying incessantly for pains which I no longer have as I am now.... Not...no, not yet....

LEIT: Piercing through this natural state, and not merely pissing away, I cut as if placing my hand inside of it, and it is self-evident.... It is whole and circular....
I am speaking now of all of it, all HERE which is encompassed. You see that, don't you?

MALOROTHUS: In a way, I do. I sense it, like a rock, the moving of a stream...a certain stream, still being formed....

LEIT: All I can do is continue this. God, it is like the never-ending dream state, HERE, with the fading...Sun....

MALOROTHUS: Something and Nothing, an Action made here....And there.... Think of what can happen here.... And I'm standing still.

LEIT: There is a pussyfooted rabbit and fox now.

MALOROTHUS: I could skip and jump.

LEIT: Pussyfooted, so it is limping about. I am awash in these showers of bliss which come from Nature's dirt.

MALOROTHUS: There is no more need.
I cannot and will not. And so I do. And so, still....

LEIT: He is being true here, now.

MALOROTHUS: A bee is buzzing alone. And it is not here, but here. And small, not giant.

LEIT: I see. He has accomplished that task or project which he had set out to complete so long ago – and abandoned even further in my memory – yet now, finished.

MALOROTHUS: I won't speak much for now, not for a while. But I must tell you that it is time for us to think, all of us. No more of this constant barrage of non-thinking as thought. I am several, divided into stones. Stones which have come from one another. I am broken apart, but do not take this to mean that I am broken. I have come apart as a stone so that, being stone, it can wash all over me and wash along my insides as well. These insides seen: they are stone. But there is more revealed. This stone of myself is different from others. This stone is sacred in a way that makes it well enough to fall apart. We all watch to see it crumble, to see the intangibility in its crumbling. It is like we are all in a dark cave, only a gleam of light comes through to shine upon this stone, we look up to watch it crumble and cake and have it fall upon us, crush our faces, fill us with pain and death, but we do not touch it, we leave it: sacred. Look at the sky.

LEIT: He is silent now.
There, I can see that soon it will be dark.
NIGHT.
Still, everything burns in comfort. Everything transformed by the light, without it it will be taken away by lack. I will still be standing in the darkness. It will be me who is nature, the rest of it gone and hidden. Night, all of us are nature. Soon....
But still, now, nature is haughtily risen, wholly risen, completely and abstractly it is all nature as this light washes over it. It is true, completely, and vindicated by the silence of Malorothus.
The animals and things which are here and which I can see if I choose to, they are all here with us as nature.
The Rabbit, the Fox, and the Bee.... All else as well, but these chosen as especially present to us, here, now. It is a mystery, something great and beyond. That is it, Mystery. All should recognize it as such....
The sun is setting now, truly. It is getting dark....
It is coming....
It is here....
NIGHT.

If you would just shut the fuck up....
No! No! No! Yes! Yes! Yes!

I have no idea what it is that is happening here. It is beyond me. I'm not controlling it. It is creating something. Something. Something else! Help me! Help me! Take me away! Get me out of here! No! I'll be trapped! Trapped forever! And ever!

(The face and arms, crying, reaching out, and falling, fading away, into distance, into darkness.)

I have done it. The fall fell. The machine stopped and stopped. A rotation goes on again. But the masseter is inflamed. Now know what has come and ended. Now know what your end is.

Indefatigable being. She, so beautiful. Fights for women. Those people I don't care for.

But her! Look at her go! It is oh so admirable. And beautiful and good, and nice to hear. For here, oh yes, here, I am triumphing ablast! Apast! Aghast! Ah yes, aghast, and forwards and on.... I fight with her song! And fight against a bit too.... I am scared, scared of you....

A crapping upon man. And the unmaking of woman. Now we might have what we wish. Only a single word needs to change for the rest to be known. Did you sit quietly, and understand? A listener is only as good as their ear. And an ear can go to war. And an ear can be killed.

What then, is heard?

A shrine was put up for Spindleshankes, my dearest friend, my greatest lover. All that he conquered (not much) was put up for the rest, to be held, to be put to the test.

He went forwards as a ghost and made peace with himself (that is, his corpse), and loved it all night.

All night, all night, none put up a fight....
Some wished and wandered, but they couldn't see the light!
They were drowned, they were shot,
By those poking prowlers....Those devious scrawlers....

The artists, again, took the night!

A baby born, another love torn, a love, a love, a pussy ripped open! A crash! A bang! The water flowed down, flowed upon, flowed away! Away! Away! The woman fell out of the shower and cracked her head open on the toilet seat. I only do what I want to do. I do not try to do anything. I cannot try. This is all I have. And the green...The Green!

Mass murder, hundred soils, a purse pussified, a trap hungered....
A towering silence, a Miserable Miser, A whore standing, a Million minding Their own business! As should you!

In the evergreen forest, the dark, wet forest, the rainforest, she cackled and trudged through it all. Yes, how clever of her.... She was to take the monkey. She was to finally take the monkey home.

And what of the power? The power 'twas there! Yas! Yas! There!

And she cried out when she saw it! Its eyes! Its eyes! What have you done to its eyes!? She was a fan of Rosemary's Baby. The monkey acted as a baby. No one understood it. Everyone wondered why.

You see, everyone is simply an automaton. We must work to become Particular Individuals with strong qualities, peculiarities, beliefs. We must be radical. Imagine if all were insane, all those we looked up to. If they suddenly became insane! How entrancing that might be.... How charismatic! Soon we would all be happily becoming like them! And how funny to see what a normal man might look like against, his face aghast, looking at *them*.

A triangle intersected (even penetrated) by a perfect rectangle. The triangle is an ugly shape. It holds such power and possibility, even meaning (and we know well enough now what that can mean). It awakens the third eye chakra, occasionally, and also drowns the viewer in dreams. It invokes mathematical probabilities and possibilities, and even drives children to murder. That is the reason for all those school shootings. That's why it should be banned. It's also just plain lewd.

All that I am. All that I will be. A pusher, a pimp, a pacifier, a player, a trap, a game, a joke, a great big joke, a liar, a truther, an artist! An artist! I am me and you are you! And what are you? What are you? I don't know you?? Don't look at me. Don't think of me. I never should have told you any of this. I never should have said a thing.

And what is it that lives? And what is it that dies? What comes here, to me, as I write this? What is moving me? The great unconscious? My newfound friend? I speak and speak and how? How do I do this? What does this all mean? It all means so much! It all means everything!

And I can go away. I am living and free and fried and died. The life leaves me and I feel my sight slip away, more than that, my energy drained from me, drained out to here, wherever here may be, I see a tree in a great land of green, yet the grass is a thousand faces all crying out at me and I am horrified! I see my face and it looks just like theirs! Do you see? Do you see? Just like theirs! My face! And theirs! And there, a little pink dollop, a man, a being, a baby infant fetus thing! And it is looking at me. And it is speaking to me, it is saying:

Christian, I'm here with you now. I'm loving you. I'm so glad you came here. To be with me.... Haha, not to be with me. But you're here now. Don't you remember? I was there, in your first poem. You can always come to see me. Maybe even in your death.... Strange little fuck, waiting for your death.... Haha, just like the rest of them.

And it did say that! It said that! It said it and it was there! And there was so much more, but I didn't have the time, no, I didn't have the time to see it all....

A masterpiece of pieces of fragments of failings of flayings of tragedy of comedy of all that you are and all that you could be and all that will be seen and all that will be known and a miniscule insect crawling up your leg tickling you and teasing you and haunting you the ghost of that insect haunting you and making you and remaking you and destroying you destroying you you know you know it is doing it to you living you through you an insect a beast a giant beast crying out to you for comfort to be held and to be loved and you are that beast to me that is what you are to me that is all you are to me and I am you and I hate me I hate you I don't know you who I am talking to who is it that is here and speaking and they interrupt me they take it away from me and what was there was now gone was all away awash awashed away from me and I write and I speak but I am happily not me not myself not anything and everything again yes again and for the founder I try to become what I must must never do never do it Never Never do it oh how beautiful words Yes Beautiful oh words come and go vibrate vigor vibrations of hollow outlanders and dowl dowlings the netterminded of the bunch who cracked and cackled and away...........

That which is real is based in the reality of the collective. This allows us much room for play within reality, for nowadays it is not so difficult to push certain groups or collectives in one direction or the other. It is not too difficult to create memes, in both senses of the world.

We have already seen this happen and so reality is easily shaped. Just think and you can know that reality is as tiny as a grape.

Black night everlasting, calling out and out again. It comes for your feelings, for your thoughts, for your sins. For it comes to make them, to take them out with them!

And don't you ever know? Don't you, my friend?

For you are a baby! One to make! And one to take! No, don't hide away, don't fool it, don't pretend.

The son went down. He went to the town. He crawled and raked, he tried to make.

Inbred father, I come to you now. Do you hear me, my Lord? As I speak to you now? I wish for something! Something new, something great! Only for Something, that Something, that sings. To sing for Something.

(Oh yes it is already here)

For something is everywhere. I feel it right here. I love it, I know it. It is inside me. And outside.
Outside us. Outside you and me.
We are careless. We are gentle. We are gentiles. We're free.

Everything and nothing. Oh God, feel me.
Hold me and know me. Make me your little bitch. For I am your slave, your poetic mistress....
Ugh. How disgusting. What a waste, what a wash. Ah, yes, but the thighs....The thoughts....Which fade all away, far and away. They make you into mincemeat. They shake you down the street. And Ms. Wort wonders for you. Yes, you remember her. She is always about. But I much prefer the Headless one. She is my cutie pie. She is the one for whom I would die.

You trollop! You pig! You masquerade! You façade!
You mask. You blade. You traitor. My skin.

My skin it blisters. It fades away and regrows. I know things because I see them, feel them, and think them. But only I can know. And only I can live. Only one person might live in a single moment, we can trade. But how Poland is so careful, so gentle, so brave....

Under the silky moon! I came oh too soon!
Under my manly mistress! I made a babe boon!

My body is a wasteland of disgust. I should die. I should live. I am not depressed. I have never once been depressed, because I say so. I'll never see a therapist. I don't like them. They're all idiots. They're all fucked themselves, that's why they became therapists. They thought maybe if they couldn't help themselves they could help others. Or that they're so fucked up they'll understand everyone else. Everyone living a false dream. Everyone lacking a dream. Lacking ambition. Everyone gone.

But we are here! And now we live! And now we know!
We are putting on the show! We are acting together, in tow!

The cuts on your body, self-inflicted, become sigils to the possibilities and impossibilities of the body. These sigils, markers, bringing you back and forth, letting the cycle recur so that you may again be everything, nothing, and yourself. These sigils, these cuts, these offerings, these sacrifices, sacrifices *to the you that you may be.*

The fantasy of removing your genitals, of removing an arm, an eye, and replacing it with another appendage. Recreating your body in your own image, in the image of the world, in the image of everything. Why do you *want* to be a man, woman, or something else when you can be *everything* else? Your appearance can become a "Universal." Your appearance itself can be all-knowing, can be beyond the boundaries of the self, beyond the subjective and objective, your appearance itself a tool for the dissolution of the "psyche."

But can it really? Does it really? How? How does your body change the world? How does it change your world? Are you hiding? Are you lying to yourself? Are you hiding from the rapes you endured? From the abuse you faced? The beatings? The names? The gaslighting? The body itself? The world calling you ugly, stupid, weak, making you face constant turmoil, forcing you to degrade yourself, to put on a show for them all? Yet, you *may* remake yourself. You may remake your *soul.* You throw away your flesh and walk about free. You throw away your morality and step onto the plane of the existential. You throw away all urges and are eviscerated. You throw away all rationality and are ready for the carcass of God.

Unbecoming

"God loves you." This is what you hope for. But God simply does whatever you wish it to do. God serves you. What do you wish for? You may make it so by invocation. By the body, by the soul, by your own world creation, you may *become*.

And yet, you are lost. These worlds, as all worlds, come to an end. Thank God that we will not know it. Thank God, it will end before our eyes, as we sleep.

I tried to tell you. I tried to tell you all that I could. I hope you listened. It might not ever happen again. It might not ever be the same. It was supposed to mean something. It was supposed to mean a lot. Piss. Shit.

Doesn't it all seem so fragile? It comes and goes. All of it.

I made a mess. Will you clean it up for me?

A majestic little creature came flying through the lands. It spoke of Hegel and Kant and Aristotle too. It seemed to know everything! But it was dying. It had been cut too deep. And its knowledge was a sham to fool others so that it could feel special. I had to let the little one go. I had to see it through.

I am glad to know nothing. I am glad to be a fool. But the world doesn't see it. The world tumbles through. I have made my own world that I am happy to live in. I have seen my own things that I am happy to do. I will come for you and take you. I'll do it to you.

Caress the cradle, rock it gently. It holds your universe, your infinity. And when you wake it, you can let it cry and shout. It is nearly time for it all to come out.

All of it, again! A thousand more! Ten thousand! A million! Soon enough a book of ten thousand shall come. And it will be a million, for some. I continue, my ambition grows. I'll give you a grove, a treasure trove, of "unwieldy masterpieces," and "disastrous controversy!" Soon you'll wish that it all came crashing, crashing down. Dance! Sing! *Play with me, thing.* Uncouple your life from that dreary little mind.

> *Blacken your heart, child. Let yourself be mine.*

Murder the mystery! Let it all be clear!

> *Hide in the shadow, wait, not in fear....*

For you are the one! The one who must be!

> *Be all over all, be the killer, be free.*

They died. They all died. And I laid in bed. I didn't even cry. I screamed. I suffered. The trees wither away. The leaves fall black. A dead crab on the beach. A sloth stomped to death. A squirrel slowly dying. An old woman's breath. My father said he hates me. My mother didn't care. My friends all abandoned me. I was left empty, there. The plane crashed. The survivors ate each other. The relationship went on and on, it couldn't end. *(All?)* And lovers hate each other. That's how all love is. And fires burn brighter when people are thrown in. And misery loves company. And people will drag you down. A little cat wheezed, and soon enough, drowned. An ugly man leered over a woman. A lonely woman stared and stared until her mind was broken. And the twin towers were struck. And many kids were killed. And manifestos are written, and assassinations made real. A child alone and hungry in the night. He cannot move, he shakes with fright. What ghost? What monster? Under the bed? Perhaps his own father, ready to sever his head.

If I die, will I be remembered? No. No one will be. Eventually we will all die. The universe will collapse. Then why am I doing this? Freedom, tyranny, my master made red dumplings and the beans were overcooked. I am doing it for myself, to experience something and to communicate my experience so that I might better understand it with others, as they might experience it as well. Communication is key for the greater man, the greater evolution, the greater devolution, I cried when the crow walked. And if I can have that while I live, well, that's about the best I can ask for, isn't it? An infinity made mice reach up to the sky. A trap card was played that gurgled my balls. A nightman watched and waited for the right moment to strike, to do it, what he'd always wanted to do. I cannot have anyone, but I will have you. Pry open the jaws. Let the steel steal us away. Come with me. Let us go to death together. I will die with you. You have read me, have you not? I will die with you. I will not die alone. I will not die alone. I will not die alone.

Night

LEIT: ...

MALOROTHUS: It is absolutely dark. He and I are oozing in it together, covered in night.

LEIT: I am absolutely oozing of night. It has been so long.

MALOROTHUS: Now I have done everything and so I now have nothing. I have gone far beyond what I once was and so my personality has collapsed. Beyond pain, beyond stone. I am here in the night with you, Leit.

LEIT: You are trying to tell me that your personality is gone and that you are now nothing, or "NIGHT" in a sense.
You've recognized that that which you create within yourself is a strong and profound sense of truth which corresponds completely with your reality, and you claim that your reality, even upon the brink of psychosis, is as valid as the whole totality of nature. Isn't that so?

MALOROTHUS: I have no time to argue. Everything is filled, I'm growing, and it is night.
My head had collapsed like the great flame and I had fallen apart like the sun.
I have said this once before, right now. Even if there is no sense, it is strong, true, and real. I can't see my hand in front of me, that's how dark it is.

LEIT: Yes, it is completely dark.

MALOROTHUS: I have reconstructed everything which I have been and I am holding it all here.
(Alas....)

LEIT: Will you be continuing on from the past?

MALOROTHUS: He doesn't see it, but there is more to it.

LEIT: After I lost him, there was nothing else I could do. It was a different time for me then, and I had thought I'd grown so much.
My limitations could never be overcome. This was just one small example of all the things I'd held on to. I can't let go of anything.
Even if I am nature, I am constantly trodden upon.
I should completely abandon myself and go further into the darkness here.
Can't I face anything? I'm horrible.
I'm just going on and on....

...

MALOROTHUS: Please, be quiet....

...

MALOROTHUS: Shhh.... Even quieter...!

...

MALOROTHUS: Look! Don't you see...?

...

LEIT: Oh! I do! I really do! I never knew it this whole time! Ha ha! Look at that! And I can see the moon!

...

MALOROTHUS: Have yourself another moment, Leit. You deserve it.
You've worked so hard and stood with me all this time. You never knew it yourself, not before now, but you were still very much a child.... But now! Just look at yourself! Look at what you've become! I'm so proud of you! Absolutely proud!

...

MALOROTHUS: Don't you have anything to say, Leit?

Anything at all?

...

MALOROTHUS: Oh, I see. He's fallen
silent. Like an imp.

...

MALOROTHUS: Awash in silence.

...

MALOROTHUS: Finagling himself.... A
rotten bastard.

...

MALOROTHUS: A whole...

...

MALOROTHUS: I do not admire you.
Nor do I admire myself.

...

MALOROTHUS: You might have been a
child, but I was an infant.

...

And they both fell completely silent.

Alone. Alone with you. And I see nothing. And it can go on. It can go on and on forever. Something about that phrase "on and on" really moves me. I like it. I can't seem to let go of it. Did you have a nice time? Did you like it? Will you tell me what you think? Please do, I want to know. I want to. I want it all.

All, and everything.... (I'm singing again)
What we do! Oh! What we do for that love! That love! We cry and we fight, my love...
We live and we die, oh love...
A tragic and swell young fright!
A beauty lost in the night!
Whether a boy or a girl,
Yes, we love...

It was supposed to be sung like a Frank Sinatra song. You will tell me, though, what you thought, won't you? I haven't forgotten. I won't forget. Life is that all-encompassing force. There are constant forces at play. There are rhythms, fluxes, thoughts. The interplay between thoughts is astounding. If you could hear it, like I can, you'd explode. Everyone is constantly thinking their own thoughts, and sometimes they align, they align perfectly, they come together and are so beautiful, sublime, perfect.... It's hard to describe. I'm sure it's hard to imagine. But that's all we can really do, imagine it. Thoughts are really pure imagination. Words aren't thoughts. These "poems" aren't thoughts. Philosophy isn't thought. Thought is pure imagination, it's inside, deep inside, and it's imagistic, but more than that, it's occultic? It's mystical, because we can't understand it. It is beautiful. It is something all encompassing, like this book. Perhaps, if you took the book all together in thought for just a moment, that is what a thought is like. But, well, you should know, you have them all the time.

Failure, that's you.

Laugh, you're a fool. I hate you. I think you're stupid. I think you wasted your time reading this. You put too much effort into getting here when you could've been doing something worthwhile, you could've been writing your own Book Of A Thousand Poems (BOATP). You shouldn't be here. You shouldn't be anywhere. You should be dead.

No life worth living.

You are mine and mine alone. But also not. Also all else. And everyone's. And your own.

 A life must be lived as though it were to end.

And it was so.
And it will be.
Forever.
You and me.

(Goodbye and hello.)

It has all been remade. There are new avenues now. Soon enough they will be explored. It was accomplished, thank God. Don't worry, you don't need to anymore. The rest is just procedure. Go ahead!

THE LAST 100 POEMS

The book was strange,
Maybe a bit of a mess,
But so beautiful
In its peculiarity
I give it all my best.

It has achieved all it set out to do,
And through this, even more...
It has rebirthed itself.
It has remade this world.

943

A bit daft
A bit dim
A bit thick
But still rich

Uncanny and uncomfortable,
Really quite horrifying.
What is there,
Within that mind?

Its commentary on capitalism
Is surely profound,
Yet all the rest
Is really quite brown.

Undeniably great.
Quaking, shaking!

947

The book made me cry,
Made me whimper,
And wonder:

Why?
Why?
Oh God,
Why?

It answered my questions
And gave me a few more.
All in all,
What more can one ask for?

949

A new organism
Was created
Through the process
Of the book.

I was happy to be included
And to have a little story,
But really, really,
I don't think I am so
That my smile is needed
To be commented upon
On and on.

Christian McDonough

The gates of Heaven can now be seen clearly,
For this book
Is all life,
Life itself,
And Death.

952

It meant so much to me!
There were times, writing it,
Where I really did feel
Truly free!

The book is nothing more
Than an assemblage of observations
On the natural world,
It's true.

It was a disaster!
How could I read it?
Not a word made sense.

955

It is my baby,
I put all I had into it.
Would you really try to kill
My baby?

It was nothing.
Just a quick game,
A cash grab,
A ploy.

The book seems to be nothing more than a joke,
But with that said,
It is among the greatest of jokes
To have ever been read.

Its satire so biting!
So clear and so true!
It has made it now clear
What we all must do.

Boring and tiring
And overly long.
How could I ever care
When it's a thousand pages long?

It speaks for itself.
Its face is a true face.
If you fall asleep too close to it
It might steal you from grace.

961

The man was good,
And nice to meet.
I would have fucked him, as was said,
But he went white as a sheet.

First and foremost
A book of philosophy,
Not poetry.
And this philosopher
Is needed,
But only for himself.

The Last 100 Poems

Christian McDonough

There wasn't
A single poem
In this
Supposed
"Book of A Thousand Poems."
What shit!

I wanted to give you an Answer.
I wanted to give you an End.
I wanted to give you Something.
Something that wasn't pretend.

965

A funny little thing
Haha
It made me laugh
It gave me a smile
It was a little gaff

966

Finally I have writ
All I have wished
And now I can sit
And wallow in this split.

967

Uncommon is this,
A book of such proportion,
Yet common enough
That you should fill
On this portion.

Laugh at it,
Throw it,
Throw it far away.
This book is for you,
For you to see,
For you to say.

969

Leit and Malorothus
Were sadly unable to attend.
They are basically stone,
Unmovable men.

The symbols
Hidden within
Are oh so obscure...
Yet so meaningful,
And tempting,
They must be unearthed!

Unduly,
Untimely,
These uncanny meditations!

Yet perfect
And gripping
For our dying nation...

Truly a patriot,
This Christian I support.
Truly a zealot,
This Christian I consort.

I hate him! I hate it!
All that he wrote!
He is evil! And empty!
He's no bloke of mine!

Perhaps we shall find,
One day,
That the Devil
Is a Christian in name...
But raised a Catholic,
A Catholic,
With an Irish surname.

A revelation!
A revolution!
A freedom of word!
It is done!
It is said!
It is beyond the absurd!

I spoke to you truthfully,
Carefully and considered,
Yet also without bounds,
Without thought,
Yet with vigor.

How careless...
How gentle...
How sour, yet sweet!
These blasphemous poems!
Nothing but a treat!

Now he may die.
He may die,
In peace.
May go away,
May finally,
Finally, feast.

979

Did you understand it?
Did you hear it?
Did you see it?
These words were all ultimate.
All ended.
All complete.

940

The Great Androgyne
Gives her thanks,
And is happy to be recognized.
She bows and curtsies,
And belches and cries.

981

And,
Perhaps now,
Or yet, soon enough...
I shall never write
Another poem:

No more fluff.

Incredible
How it went on
And on
And on
And grew
And grew

983

Poems mean nothing,
Or at least they did...
Yet now they are everything.
All that I meant.

A book for Poles,
Yet not in their language.
I hope that someday
It will be translated.

My brothers!
My sisters!
I call to you now!
Please buy a copy!
Or I'll send you one
Anyhow!

Gongoflesh lives on
And fucks forever more.

His brother Hongo,
Half unfleshed,
Still complains of sores.

987

A shattered diamond,
A fractalized experience...

Yet unified
And together:
The ultimate coherence.

Now to become
All that I am.
To throw this book away
And free myself
Again.

None of it matters,
Not a word that was said.
But in between each...
Through what is not said...
A perfect thing...may emerge!

Christian McDonough

A divine book!
A book of the lord!
Holy God,
Would surely smile,
And surely did,
As it was written...

Women trapped in loveless marriages
Will surely read it
And find love again...
Self-love, of course,
But with that comes changes.

It is a book.
That is
What it is.

993

A book
Of a thousand
Poems

994

My gesammtkunstwerk
Yes, *the* gesammtkunstwerk!

Fuck you! Wagu!

An experiential excursion
Upon a path
Never before taken.

A self-fulfilling project.
That is,
A project in which
The writer's self
Is the central subject
And is, throughout,
Continuously fulfilled.

Blakeley and Blaureene
Are happily nowhere to be seen.
But I wonder,
Might they read it?
And what would they then see?

A child's plaything,
A child's scribble.
Truly childlike
And free.

999

A little,
Actually, a rather large,
Menagerie
Of Thought.

1000

For you
This was everything,
For it was all
For you.

1001

A place of being.
A place within which
One can be.

A sacrifice
To some
Obscure
Forgotten
God.

A new Book,
A new Holy Book.
A Scripture
From which
All will learn
And live
As they should.

A hidden manifesto,
Not only for life,
But for society.
And a message
For those
In power.

A total philosophy
Which shapes the world
And changes it.

It is the final statement
Of poetry.
Now none
Need be done.

1007

A wild goose chase
For meaning!

India, my love,
Is right here, and happy.
I hope an everlove
Our love might be.

 The Last 100 Poems

1009

A deceiver,
A charlatan,
A fool,

Oh my!

All this and more
In that spine
Unified.

An empty casket
Waiting to be filled.
An unmarked grave
Ready to be robbed.

A response to the great thinkers.
A challenge, too.
For this book will overcome them
As soon as it overcomes you.

Those metaphysical feelings
Do wash over me,
Here and there,
As I read it.
Good job!
I'm proud of you.
Yes, you did it.

1013

You have read,
You have learned,
You have spoke,
You have been.
I hope you really feel
That I am now
Your friend.

It spits in the face of any poet that reads it.
It has no care, no respect, for the medium it claims to be a part of.

A smiling woman,
That's what it is.
And it speaks too,
And listens.

An odd kind of guru,
The bastard seems to think himself.
Let's turn away from him
And I'll show you something else.

I have *witnessed* it all
And I must say,
"Pretty good!"

It clearly wasn't meant to make sense
And must have had very little thought behind it,
Because it said insane things.

And I fell before it
In prayer...

Christian McDonough

It killed my daughter.
I don't know how,
But it killed her.
So, because of that,
I can't really say that I liked it...
But still,
It was amazing.

Blaine is around,
I'll see him soon enough.
I'll give him a good talking to,
He always needs it,
He's so rough.

1021

It violated my soul
And helped me to realize
That I am a woman
Trapped in a man's body.

So, there's that.

It seems to understand
The shadow government
Which controls us (of course),
But I don't get
All the shit
About freedom.

So sweet! So sweet!
I walk across the lands within it.
And I would smile,
Smile so much,
If only I could.

Congratulations!

If you made it
All the way
Then you have seen
All that my life
Has been
Up to now.

The Last 100 Poems

It maybe said too much
Or somehow too little,
But that fighting spirit
Can't help but overcome!

My life has ended
Due to this dire book.
For now there is nothing
Left to do,
No rhyme
Nor reason.
Only me, here, with it.

1027

An undulating mass of tentacles and cells
Which grow and multiply.
And the thing has thousands of eyes.
You can't see it if you look,
But you'll know it
If you try.

A book for all
And a book for none.
Mostly, though,
It's plain old fun.

My mother
And my father
Maybe don't need to read
This book of obscenities,
Of disasters and schemes.

It's like a pirate.
And it has invaded my ship
And stole all the booty.
And I'm sore, so sore,
From all that it has done.

A product of our times,
A product.

Only now
Could something
Of this sort
Be made...

It is a thing
Only to be held
And used,
Like a pillow.

It was a tragedy.
Like a Greek tragedy?
That is true.

An Answer
To all questions
And an End
To all thought

1035

A child
For you
To care for

996

1036

I couldn't have done it
Without all this life.

And your life
And my life
Are together
Entangled
Forever.

A plant
A plant life
Life
A life

An insect
A mammal
A person
A tool

1039

It is Everything
And
Nothing.

On this,
Our last day,
My shit hath turned Green.

Alas, perhaps again...
I shall never be seen.

www.ingramcontent.com/pod-product-compliance
Lightning Source LLC
Chambersburg PA
CBHW060856140726
47996CB00001B/1